# INSIDE OUTSIDE BROADCASTS

*Robert Hudson*

Best wishes,

Robert Hudson

28.10.91°

R & W Publications (Newmarket) Ltd.

ISBN 0951660454

Cover design by K. E. Walden of R & W Publications (Newmarket) Ltd.
Typeset and published by R & W Publications (Newmarket) Ltd.,
Goodwin House, Willie Snaith Road, Newmarket, Suffolk CB8 7SQ
Printed by Halstan and Co. Ltd., Amersham, Bucks.

_For Barbara_

Dear Reader

All the royalties from _Inside Outside Broadcasts_ will be given to **Cancer Relief Macmillan Fund** in memory of Barbara Hudson, who died of cancer in 1987.

I am sure you will find this book full of interest and amusement, and in buying it, you will be supporting my favourite charity, which helps over 150,000 people with cancer every year.

The Marchioness of Zetland
President of Cancer Relief Macmillan Fund

# CONTENTS

# Preface

To be able to write this Introduction is a dividend from my years as a fellow-toiler and friend of Robert Hudson, who has long hidden his individual light under a bushel, even though his broadcasts have burnt brilliantly. Now we have him, at last, telling the professional life story of one of the best, most dependable, and hitherto the most self-effacing of commentators. My Preface seeks to give him a laurel garland – a Hudson's bay of honour.

As I had myself started, years earlier, Bob began his staff career after the Second World War in the BBC's eminent North Region, provincial seed-plot of national success, where he became adept both at the microphone and the backstage desk as Head of Administration. That experience armoured him for the period 1969 to 1975, his most important years of service which were spent at Broadcasting House, London. He had become radio's Head of Outside Broadcasts, masterminding everything from Olympic Games coverage to the Investiture of the Prince of Wales, and the entire reconstruction of the corporation's radio sports output. He was the most meticulous manager the Department had ever known. He was involved in television's pioneer days, too.

But it was to the world 'listening to the wireless' that he became known and admired, a vivid and immaculate describer of events. You felt you were on the spot, by his side, as his words, salted by pertinent darts of humour, pictured the scenes of countless great occasions.

As well as his skill, listeners could sense his knowledge and pride of tradition. Not that he daubed scenes with hyperbole or grandiloquence: his sentences were spoken in level, robust and immediately clear English, consummately timed, letting the natural sounds of the events proclaim themselves. He has never been one of those talkers who obstructively get between the public and the pageantry.

And every one of those exactly-informed commentaries – their flow sounding so easy and so natural – was founded on prodigious homework, which sometimes meant all-night research and the fashioning of his special prompt-note cards.

Turn the following pages slowly. They are vintage Hudson, lovely to read. Don't miss the Churchill funeral ('a massive display of gratitude') or the joys of the chapter called 'Eventful Days'. The book stands as a fascinating facet of the history of broadcasting itself.

Godfrey Talbot LVO, OBE

# Foreword

## Bob of All Trades

I am delighted to write a Foreword to Robert Hudson's long-overdue story of his varied forty-five years of broadcasting.

I must immediately declare an interest. He is an old friend and colleague, and it was he, as Head of Outside Broadcasts, who so kindly invited me to join *Test Match Special* in 1970, when I was discarded by TV. So I have always been grateful to him for that.

He was the most unsung commentator, and, with his modest and unassuming character, certainly the least extrovert of us all. His research, preparation and sheer hard work put us all to shame. And he made it all sound so easy!

He had a quiet friendly voice which nudged interesting titbits of information to you without thrusting it down your throat. He was observant and quick to notice odd happenings which lighten a broadcast.

He deserves the title of 'Bob of all trades' because of his versatility – Royal Occasions, Ceremonials like Trooping the Colour and the Cenotaph Service, Royal Tours, and even one *Down Your Way*! I worked with him on many of the big occasions but knew him best from our happy days together in the cricket commentary box for both television and radio. We always called him the lucky commentator because he seemed to be on the air for most of the exciting moments.

Without going over the top (like some of us) he always managed to portray the tension and excitement to listeners. Both in cricket and rugby football he took tremendous pains to absorb the records and details of all the players, as well as having a deep knowledge of the laws and techniques of both games.

Good luck, Bob, with this book. I hope its sales approach the number of broadcasts you made over the last forty-five years.

Brian Johnston CBE, MC

# Introduction

In this book I have tried to give readers an insight into the world of broadcasting and to take them behind the scenes of some of the most memorable and important events in the history of radio and television. I believe that, after 45 years as a broadcaster, including six years as Head of Radio Outside Broadcasts for the BBC, my variety of experience is unequalled by anybody else in this field.

I was very much a child of the wireless. In 1924, at the age of four, headphones clamped to my ears and with my brother tuning in the 'cat's whisker', I heard the first ever Royal broadcast. This was the opening of the Wembley Exhibition by King George V – appropriately on St George's Day.

Years later, during the Second World War, I trained in England with the 6th Regiment Royal Horse Artillery and became something of an expert on the control of large-scale artillery fire by radio. My superior officers seemed to think that I had a clear voice and a good grasp of the complicated wireless drill needed for the transmission of orders. It seemed to me that these attributes might appeal to the BBC after the war.

Evidently they did. Rather to my surprise, my request for an audition as a cricket commentator was granted and, at the second attempt, I was passed fit for public consumption. Television, too, tried me out on rugby. All this resulted in spasmodic employment on a freelance basis.

In the late forties, when television had not yet reached the Midlands, I found myself taking the sleeper south from Kilmarnock to televised rugby matches in the London area. Later, conversely, I would travel from London to Manchester and Leeds for cricket on the radio. I always seemed to be going in the opposite direction!

Eventually, in January 1954, the BBC thought it expedient to take me on full-time as the Senior Outside Broadcasts Producer in the North Region and so started twenty-one years on the BBC staff and many more after that as a freelance. This position led to posts in Administration and Management; also to commentating, on both TV and radio, at countless National and International Events, including Sport, Royal Ceremonies and State Occasions, at home and abroad.

In this book, I re-live some of the public and sporting events which remain most vividly in my mind.

My thanks are due to Jan Wade and Katheryn Walden of R & W Publications; also to Roger George Clark for his photographic expertise and to

Peter Coombs for drawing the cartoons.

No two people could better represent the main strands of the book, the broadcasting of Public Events and Sport, than my BBC colleagues of many years' standing, Godfrey Talbot and Brian Johnston. I am most grateful to them for contributing the Preface and Foreword respectively.

Last, but by no means least, my thanks to Diana Dean, who deciphered my handwriting, typed the manuscript and gave much sound advice.

Be my guest in the commentary box. My hope is that memories will be stirred, if you are older, and interest awakened if you are young; above all, I hope that you will enjoy it.

Robert Hudson
St Albans, September 1992

# CHAPTER 1

# Early Days: How Broadcasting Began

" This is two Emma Toc calling; Eckersley, Writtle, calling."

It was 14th February 1922, exactly nine months before the first day's broadcasting by the 'British Broadcasting Company'. A young man was speaking into a microphone from a small hut in the village of Writtle, near Chelmsford, in Essex. His name was Peter Eckersley.

Eckersley was a brilliant engineer, leading a talented and innovative team from the Marconi Company. Marconi had been authorised, by the Postmaster General, to broadcast a weekly half-hour programme 'for the benefit of the Wireless Societies' – a growing army of amateur enthusiasts, most of whom had built their own sets.

One of these enthusiasts was Robert Wood, listening with such tense excitement, in his Sheffield attic, that he was late for his evening classes; he was in his final year as an apprentice in electrical engineering with Cammell Laird. Ahead of Wood, although he could hardly have guessed it, lay forty years of close involvement in great occasions of State and memorable moments in our history.

Eckersley and Wood were soon to meet and, each in his own way, to play key roles in British broadcasting. Eckersley became the Chief Engineer of the BBC but, sadly, his brilliant brain was only available to the BBC for six years. He was then cited in a divorce petition and promptly sacked by Reith. Things were different in those days.

To R. T. B. Wynn, another member of Eckersley's Marconi team who also eventually became Chief Engineer of the BBC, we are indebted for the following account of life at Writtle on Tuesdays, which was 'programme day': 'On Tuesday afternoon, the piano would be trundled into the hut and we would receive a bunch of records – most of them usually rejected as too highbrow. Programme planning was done at the Cock and Bell up the road. We had artistic ambitions – for example we put on *Cyrano de Bergerac,* the first play ever to be broadcast... Our star was Eckersley'.

Peter Eckersley was much more than an engineer: he was an actor, a comedian and a singer as well. He would conclude the half-hour programme, in his high tenor voice, with this theme song:

> Dearest, the concert's ended, sad wails the heterodyne.
> You must switch off your valves, I must switch off mine.
> Write back and say you heard me, your 'hook-up', where and how
> Quick! for the engine's failing; goodbye you old low-brow.

The Writtle broadcast continued once a week for about a year, until January 1923, and Marconi had also been allowed to start a new station, 2LO, from Marconi House in the Strand. With the encouragement and help of *The Daily Mail* and its founder and owner, Lord Northcliffe, 2LO broadcast a boxing commentary on 11th May 1922; the fight was Kid Lewis v Georges Carpentier at Olympia. On 7th October, the Prince of Wales came to the studio to broadcast a message to the Boy Scouts; this was the first ever Royal Broadcast.

Meanwhile, not only Marconi, but other great companies like General Electric and Ferranti, were realising the enormous potential of the 'wireless'. The newspapers, however, except *The Daily Mail,* were apprehensive lest the rise of this new medium should destroy their sales. So conflict was in the air. Representatives of six of the biggest electric companies, and of many smaller ones as well, met on 18th October 1922 and formed the British Broadcasting Company. It had a share capital of £100,000 and was charged with the task of producing programmes. An office was provided at Magnet House in Kingsway and the studio, a few hundred yards away in Mansion House, was used to launch the first BBC programme on 14th November 1922.

There was a staff of four: Peter Eckersley (Chief Engineer), Arthur Burrows (Head of Programmes), C.A. Lewis (Assistant Head of Programmes) and P.F. Anderson (Company Secretary). They seem to have spent their time rushing madly from office to studio. Arthur Burrows started by reading the News, received from the News Agencies, first at normal pace and then again, slowly, "so that you can take notes". The microphone was a wooden box-like structure on wheels. On one occasion, a small soprano came to sing and they stood her on a pile of books. On reaching the top note, the books collapsed, and she was retrieved from under the piano. Thus, the BBC took to the air.

It is particularly unfortunate that Lord Northcliffe who, through *The Daily Mail,* had done much to foster broadcasting in the early days, and had persuaded Dame Nellie Melba to sing from the very first experimental Marconi station at Chelmsford in 1920, did not quite live to see the BBC in action.

When Robert Wood finished his apprenticeship he was promoted at Cammell Laird, but his burning ambition was to join the BBC. He wrote, applying for a job, and was seen in London by Peter Eckersley, whose voice had entranced him in his attic in Sheffield. He also met Mr J.C.W. Reith, the high-principled Scot, who had recently been appointed General Manager at the age of thirty-three. In his 'office', no more than a curtained-off cubicle, Reith, at six feet six inches tall, fixed Wood with penetrating eyes. 'It made me feel like a couple of threepenny bits', Wood later wrote in his memoirs. Incidentally, Winston Churchill's name for Reith was 'Wuthering Heights'. Whatever you called him, the architect of British Broadcasting was in place by the end of 1922 and the BBC was on its way.

The interview was a success and Wood was duly appointed Engineer in Charge of the new station, 2ZY, in Manchester. He was nineteen years and nine months old.

The station was in an old warehouse in Dickenson Street. It had a small studio from which Dan Godfrey, wearing a rugger jersey, would conduct a talented group of musicians, including some members of the Hallé Orchestra. The transmitter was on the roof. The cramped conditions encouraged Wood to seek new pastures outside the studio; thus began Outside Broadcasting in Manchester. The BBC had little money for new technology. It received only half the ten shilling licence fee, so it was forced to acquire microphones, valves and batteries on credit, in order to assemble the 'OB' equipment needed.

The cinema in Oxford Road had an orchestra, which played between the films. Wood persuaded the Post Office to run a line back to the studio and the first OB in the North took to the air. Other orchestras followed, from the Midland Hotel, and eventually the Hallé itself, from the Free Trade Hall – all done with one microphone! Live sports broadcasts, as in London, were outlawed by the Press and News Agencies, who were supplying the BBC with news. Such broadcasts, they felt, would damage the sale of newspapers.

Nevertheless, broadcasting was having an effect on people's lives. Although the letters 'BBC' had yet to open any doors, reputations were being made, particularly those of composers and musicians; 'song- pluggers', too, were soon in evidence.

The very first Outside Broadcast by the BBC was a relay of *The Magic Flute* from Covent Garden on 8th January 1923. It was followed, a month later, by *Cinderella* from the London Hippodrome. For these initiatives we have to thank Roger, Peter Eckersley's brother, who succeeded Arthur Burrows as Head of Programmes.

In April 1923, the Queen Mother married the Duke of York. There was no broadcast of the wedding. The Dean of Westminster had decided that the "new fangled wireless" could not be allowed because "people might be listening to it in public houses with their hats on". How times change. Some sixty years on, a later Dean of Westminster, the Very Reverend Michael Mayne, was a former Head of BBC Religious Broadcasting.

By the time 1924 was ushered in by the first broadcast of the chimes of Big Ben, there were 177 on the staff and the BBC had moved into offices and studios in part of the Institute of Electrical Engineers building in Savoy Hill. John Reith and the Eckersley brothers had, in one year, set a steady course for the future.

Gerald Cock became the first Head of Outside Broadcasts in 1925. His job, at the time, must have been frustrating because the BBC still had no News Department of its own and was at the mercy of the News Agencies and the Press, who refused to allow live sports broadcasts. The situation changed dramatically in the following year.

On 30th April 1926, a broadcast by Jack Payne's Dance Band was interrupted for an announcement that a General Strike would start on 4th May. It lasted eight days and changed the face of British Broadcasting.

Suddenly there were no newspapers.

The BBC acted quickly and created a News Department, working a three-shift system. The News Agencies continued to supply news and the BBC appointed its own reporters for the first time. Five bulletins were broadcast throughout the day, instead of only between 7.00pm and 11.00pm as hitherto, and the BBC maintained a precarious measure of independence, under extreme pressure from the Government. Reith was 36 years old. It was his finest hour. He had no sympathy with either the coal owners, or the miners, whose dispute had precipitated the General Strike, but was determined to uphold the editorial independence of the BBC.

When the Prime Minister, Stanley Baldwin, broadcast during the strike, Reith persuaded him to insert the words, 'I am a man of peace. I am longing and working and praying for peace, but I will not surrender the safety and security of the British Constitution'.

The Government had been considering the future of Broadcasting before the strike took place. Two million people had bought the ten-shilling licence. Its importance could no longer be questioned. It would clearly become the most important and essential means of communication. On 1st January 1927 the BBC became a Corporation by Royal Charter and threw off the shackles of the Press and News Agencies. The era of outside broadcasting and the 'running commentary', as it came to be called, had dawned. Television was still nine years away.

By 1927, Robert Henry Wood, generally known as 'RH', was working in London and was in charge of the technical side of a rash of sporting and other broadcasts.

With their new-found freedom, Gerald Cock and his assistant, Lance Sieveking, who together constituted the Outside Broadcasts Department, set to with a will. Although wary of the new medium, the sporting authorities were prepared to give it a trial. Thus Wood, who had little interest in sport, found himself driving his OB van to Twickenham on 15th January 1927 for the Rugby International between England and Wales. It was the first sporting commentary by the BBC. Admission to the terraces was two shillings and sixpence (12½p) and England won 11 – 9. The only advice given to the

*Outside Broadcasts rig for the BBC's first live running commentary broadcast – England vs Wales international rugby match at Twickenham, 15 January 1927.*

commentator, Captain H. B. T. Wakelam, was two words written on a card propped against the microphone. They were: 'Don't Swear'!

Live OBs of the Grand National, Wimbledon and the Boat Race followed in the same year, as did the World Snooker Final which was won by Joe Davis for a prize of six pounds and ten shillings. Football commentaries flourished with George Allison wedging his ample frame into the small portable commentary boxes. Cricket, on the other hand, as I recount in the chapter 'Test Match Special', was slow to gain acceptance on the air.

At the Boat Race, having no two-way link from launch to shore, Wood looked for a white handkerchief, waved from the roof of Harrods Depository, which served as a transmitting point, to confirm that the broadcast was getting through.

Outside Broadcasts of Trooping the Colour, the Cenotaph Service and the Lord Mayor's Banquet became hardy annuals, as did visits to seaside towns like Margate and Eastbourne for concerts and other entertainment. Essentially, the events that made Outside Broadcasting have not changed; sport, Royal ceremonies and State occasions are still given major coverage, and the seaside concerts have their modern counterparts in programmes like *Radio 4 Goes to Town* and the *Radio 1 Roadshow*.

The importance of outside broadcasting was growing all the time and Wood gradually acquired adequate staff to support him. However, he continued to handle the important occasions himself. His close association with the Royal Family began in 1932 when he put King George V on the air for the first Christmas Broadcast from Sandringham. Afterwards, the King wrote in his diary: 'Broadcasted 251 words to the Empire'. A meticulous monarch!

The King's Silver Jubilee in 1935 was the last big test for radio on its own, before the arrival of television the following year. Wood remained loyal to radio and, for nearly three more decades, was at the centre of a series of momentous events.

The abdication of the uncrowned king, Edward VIII, the Coronations of King George VI and Queen Elizabeth II, the outbreak of war and Churchill's wartime speeches were all covered by radio in the next seventeen years. A common thread through all these was the presence of Robert Wood.

The Abdication speech of Edward VIII was made on 11th December 1936

Above: *R. H. Wood (left) and H. J. Gregory on board 'Magician' transmitting commentary on Oxford and Cambridge Boat Race to Harrod's Depository (Left).*

from a study in the Augusta Tower at Windsor Castle. According to Wood, the King looked 'quite normal and not in the least at the end of his tether'. He was introduced by Sir John Reith who, apparently, knocked his foot against a table leg; listeners telephoned the BBC to ask why the Director-General had "stormed out of the room and slammed the door"! The monarch resigned his inherited position with the words, "I have found it impossible to carry the heavy burden of responsibility and to discharge my duties as King, as I would wish to do, without the help and support of the woman I love" (Mrs Wallis Simpson). After the broadcast, the Royal Daimler 'whizzed out of the gates to the coast, and so to France'.

Before the Coronation of King George VI in 1937, Wood was sent to Buckingham Palace to familiarise the King with the use of a microphone and to do what he could to cure the monarch of his stutter. Thus began a close and friendly association with the King and Queen, whom he always held in high esteem.

The night before the Coronation, Wood was asked to sleep in the Abbey 'so as not to be run over by a bus'. A camp bed was installed in a small store room next to the Control Point. However, each time Wood nodded off, he was woken up again by Big Ben striking the quarter hour; he spent most of the night wandering about the Abbey in his pyjamas. In the morning he had to mix the output of fifty-eight microphones, some hidden in flowers and chandeliers, and one in each arm of Edward the Confessor's Chair. Furthermore, he had to do it 'blind', without a television monitor. Television, having been refused permission to televise from within the Abbey, had placed their only three cameras at Hyde Park Corner. The King and Queen were asked to smile at them, "if you find it convenient".

Later in the same year, Wood found himself on board HMS Nelson at Spithead. Tommy Woodroffe was to broadcast a Review of the Fleet by the King and Queen. The fleet was in line ahead and, as dusk fell, was decorated with lights. Tommy was a former naval officer and the reunion with his old shipmates had been celebrated in some style. From his broadcasting position in the captain's swivel chair on the bridge, Tommy Woodroffe made the point, not once but several times, that the "fleet's lit up". So it was – but so was he. Swinging round in the chair, he announced that "the fleet's all gone – disappeared!". So had the broadcast – it had been faded out. Subsequently, a musical comedy called *The Fleet's Lit Up* ran for many months in London.

On 3rd September 1939, Robert Wood was at 10 Downing Street. At eleven o'clock the Prime Minister, Neville Chamberlain, was to broadcast to the nation. He was still hoping for a message from Adolf Hitler; the alternative was war.

Eleven o'clock came and went. Chamberlain would not begin and the minutes ticked by. Eventually, Wood, bombarded by calls from Broadcasting House, approached Chamberlain and said, "Sir, the world is waiting". Chamberlain looked at him: "Very well, we will make the announcement now". He spoke briefly in a doleful voice, ending with the fateful words "...consequently this country is at war with Germany".

With television shut down, nothing did more to lift morale during the war than the incomparable radio broadcasts of Winston Churchill. On every occasion Robert Wood was the engineer. Churchill prepared very thoroughly for his broadcasts, but took the view that he would start when he was ready – not at the convenience of the BBC.

Many of his broadcasts were made from 10 Downing Street, but some from the underground War Room off Whitehall. They were always

*Winston Churchill broadcasts at 3 o'clock, Tuesday 8th May, 1945, that the war with Germany has been won.*

'live', but often, perhaps only three minutes before going on the air, Churchill was nowhere to be seen. He would usually be found in the Map Room next to his bedroom-cum-study, where the broadcasts were made.

Having been extracted from the entourage of Admirals and Generals, he would settle behind the microphones (there were always two lines in case one was bombed or sabotaged) and want to start at once. A typical exchange would be to this effect:

Wood:        Prime Minister, first you will hear Big Ben for nine o'clock.
Churchill:   They all know the time. We can do without that.
Wood:        Then you have to be announced.
Churchill:   But they all know me...

Then on would go the green light and out would come that wonderful voice and those rolling sentences which would inspire the whole nation.

Afterwards, Wood and Churchill would have a glass of whisky together and the great man would give his young engineer a cigar as a memento of the occasion.

After the war, the King awarded the MVO to R. H. Wood at a private audience in 1946. When the King died in 1952, Wood was invited to the funeral, in St George's Chapel, Windsor, as a private individual, but preferred to remain in charge of the broadcast.

I knew RH in his later years and worked with him on many occasions, including the marriage of Princess Margaret and Lord Snowdon in 1960. Nobody who knew him would forgive me for neglecting to refer to the famous malapropisms, or 'Woodisms', to which he was exceptionally prone. Talking about one of his staff, he created a classic culinary mix-up: "Well, the proof of the pigeon is in the eating; he's buttered his bread, now he must lie on it".

Robert Henry Wood was just as much an integral part of the early days of broadcasting as were the Eckersley brothers and the towering figure of the Director General, Sir John Reith. Moreover, he was a 'character', who put history on the air.

# CHAPTER 2

# Describe it this way

"Paint a picture and keep it the right way up".

So said Wilfred Rhodes, the famous Yorkshire and England cricketer. He was talking to me about radio commentaries, as we sat on a sofa at his home in Huddersfield. He was old and blind but his brain was clear and his views succinct and forthright.

That interview took place in the 1950s when television had only just reached the North of England.

For television, the commentator annotates a picture which is already there. On the radio, he creates one. The difference is total. All that they have in common is the need for preparation.

Seymour de Lotbinière ('Lobby'), who was six feet seven inches tall, was striding about his office thumping his right fist into the palm of his left hand. Lobby was Head of BBC Radio Outside Broadcasts from 1935 to 1940 and again for some years after the war when, for a time, television was also under his wing. He had legal training and a penetrating mind. To him we owe the original conceptual thinking about radio and TV commentary. Prior to his arrival, people just talked and hoped for the best. Some still do.

Blaring out of a loudspeaker in Lobby's office was my own first radio 'audition', a twenty-minute recorded commentary on a cricket match at Lords in 1946. From time to time Lobby, no particular cricket enthusiast himself, would stop the recording: "You say Jones is bowling from the Pavilion End – but where is the Pavilion? I get no picture from that. What does Jones look like? You don't tell us".

I grew steadily more miserable, yet fascinated by the clinical dissection. It was a new world.

As I tottered out of the office, with the promise of a further audition, his secretary soothed my nerves: "Don't worry", she said, "Lobby never wastes time on duds".

Lobby was formulating the grammar of a language – the technique of commentary. We have all met foreigners who speak total rubbish in a passable English accent. No doubt we are equally guilty ourselves. Similarly, there are those on the air with a glib fluency but who paint no picture in the mind. They have not learned the 'grammar'.

In broadcasting, a rugby match is a journey into the unknown whereas a Royal Wedding is a set piece occasion where the pattern of events should unfold as planned. The grammar of the commentary language is exactly the same for both.

Essential basic facts come first: "England won the toss and have made 83 for one wicket". Then the 'big picture' – "a full house at Lords on a bright sunny day" – into which the action will be placed and woven together with the background, so that a complete picture is built up.

Within the first half-minute, establish your position in relation to the event you are describing. You may be looking "across the half-way line" or "up the Nave from the West Gallery towards the Altar". You keep the listener firmly behind your eyes and describe the scene consistently in relation to your own position, ie "Keep it the right way up", as Wilfred Rhodes advised.

In cricket, the commentator is usually "behind the bowler's arm"; but the bowler may be bowling from either end of the pitch. So he can be running "away from" or "towards" the commentator. These words create a clearer picture than, for example, "from the New Road end" – helpful only to those who know where New Road is.

Action is sacrosanct, so don't miss it! Take your eyes off the ball and that is the one that will take a wicket. Make the most of 'suspense interest' in sport. You don't know what is going to happen next, and nor do your listeners.

Use your 'associative material', all those facts so lovingly collected, in exactly the right place. During an audition at a rugby match, one hopeful candidate, anxious to display his homework, even though a wing three-quarter was racing for the try line, yelled into the microphone, "He's a dentist and lives in Ealing". Hardly what we wanted to know at that moment, but interesting if a player had a tooth knocked out.

Make life easy for your listener (and it is best to think of *one* person; perhaps someone doing the washing-up in Surbiton or driving up the M1); do the mental arithmetic at cricket matches or signpost ahead to the next hymn at the Royal Wedding. If the ball goes into touch, pinpoint the spot – "on the far side of the field, the England left, ten yards inside the Welsh half". Keep up the 'geography', so that, with paper and pencil, it is possible to follow the ball. In the old days, a plan of the field was printed in *Radio Times* and divided into squares. Nowadays, the commentator must obviate the need for the solemn voice intoning "square four".

Names are all very well and instant recognition is essential, but give a cricketer a mop of red hair and a cap slightly askew, and he begins to come to life. Lists of names, titles and decorations read out in full are the kiss of death to a commentary. They will all be in your ceremonial document, but resist the temptation. Concentrate on the key figures and, with a vivid word or two, give a general impression of the scene – and forget the rest.

Leaving our radio commentator for a moment, let us glance next door into the rather more spacious apartment of his television counterpart.

The television OB producer was, in my experience, mainly concerned with his cameras and how to deploy them to the best advantage, and the comfort and well-being of his commentator was low on his agenda. The engineers were busy with thousands of technical matters and the commentator, dumped in some dusty gallery with a monitor screen, which may or may not work, and with no table for his notes, usually felt himself to be just what he was – merely an adjunct to the picture.

Yet he can make or mar the broadcast. Few would dispute that Richard Dimbleby's commentary on the Coronation in 1953, for example, was crucial to the success of the broadcast.

Let us assume that things have improved. Our commentator has a desk, a comfortable chair and at least two monitor screens; one will show him the picture being transmitted, the other, probably, the next picture in line for

*Tom Fleming commentating on the Silver Jubilee of Queen Elizabeth II.*

transmission. From his headphones he hears, in one ear, the voice of the producer in the OB van giving instructions to the cameramen and, occasionally, to him; in the other ear is the sound of the event itself. So his ears are on overtime, as are his eyes which dart between the picture, the event and his notes.

The television commentator's job is entirely different to that of the radio commentator. He does not need to paint a picture; it is already there. In that respect, his life is easier. On the other hand, he has the infinitely difficult task of drawing out of any given picture what is not immediately clear, but is of relevant interest. He has to think in a missing dimension, avoiding the obvious. If in doubt, he should keep quiet.

People tend to say, of some television commentators, "Oh, he talks too much – why doesn't he shut up?" And yet those same people will listen to a continuous radio commentary while watching the television picture, indicating that they want *more* talk rather than less! The answer is that a television commentator can talk *all* the time, if he can consistently add to your knowledge of the picture. Richard Dimbleby talked almost non-stop on State Occasions, but nobody complained; Bill MacLaren does much the same at rugby matches. Peter Alliss illuminates golf, in a magical way, for a non-golfer like myself. I can recognise Nick Faldo, but what club is he using and why? Look at the position of his feet as he prepares to drive; where is he aiming to land the ball? What are the hazards of this hole, and how long is it? Peter Alliss tells me all this, and I am grateful. He is adding to the picture and to my enjoyment.

Television commentary abroad is hazardous. You can feel lost without an

English producer whispering in your ear. A foreigner is controlling the cameras. You have been briefed as to his intentions, but these don't always materialise. You are out on a limb but with Big Brother watching from London.

"This has been most moving", said the London voice in 1961, "we will carry on to the cemetery". It was the funeral of Dag Hammarskjöld, Secretary General of the United Nations, at Uppsala in Sweden. His coffin was being carried out of the Cathedral. I was the TV commentator and had been 'adding to the picture' with some success so far. This should have been the end of the programme, so the edict from London was not welcome.

A slow march through the streets of Uppsala, about which I knew nothing, lay ahead. Luckily, a girl from Swedish Television, who was with me, had a guidebook, albeit written in Swedish. She was able to recognise some landmarks and translate them for me into English, so I maintained an outwardly confident front, which concealed a sinking heart. Things were made worse by the positioning of the Swedish cameras at the ends of streets, so that the sober-suited mourners, following the coffin, always appeared to be coming towards you. The only figure I recognised was Mrs Pandit, sister of the first Prime Minister of India after Independence, and herself later the first woman President of the United Nations General Assembly. Consequently, she was mentioned five times, and must rank as the most dogged mourner of all time. I fear I buried Dag Hammarskjöld with indecent haste, before the voice in London had any further bright ideas.

Preparation consists of reading, talking, watching and making notes. Success in the hazardous business of live commentary depends almost entirely on preparation. To say it is ninety per cent of the battle is no exaggeration. Confidence at the microphone is built on it and confidence is everything.

In radio, the commentator has the shape of the commentary in his own hands. He can decide what to talk about and when. If he doesn't recognise people, he can usually avoid mentioning them – unless, of course, they are about to score a try, hit a six, or get married. In television, the commentator is at the mercy of the producer and the picture he decides to transmit.

A producer thinks in visual terms and tries to achieve the best possible picture. Therefore, if the commentator is not to be caught out, his knowledge must be encyclopaedic and his preparation even more thorough than for radio.

Background reading is important, whether about a Cathedral or a football match. You cannot talk to too many people, although you soon discover which are likely to be useful. Lord Mayors and Archbishops tend to know little of the detail; a junior secretary, however, may turn out to have the seating plans for the Banquet, and the Sacrist will know all about a Royal Wedding. At Trooping the Colour, the Brigade Major and the Garrison Sergeant Major will probably be able to provide more useful information than the Commanding Officer.

Before rugby matches, telephone the printer of the programme to get the numbers on the players' jerseys; the Club Secretary may well tell you from memory and get it wrong. Get proof copies of ceremonial documents; the final versions usually appear at the last moment, particularly at funerals. Too late to be of use to you.

Attend rehearsals, however sketchy, watch the rugby practice, on that cold club ground, and see the cricketers at the nets, if you can. Then disentangle the jumble of notes in your notebook, marshal them in the way you want them, and stick them on cardboard. That way they won't rustle or blow away.

It is essential that your commentary position is as you want it, with the desk at the right height and TV monitor at the right angle. Sit there and imagine the scene as it will be on the day. Try to get a good night's sleep prior to the event and arrive at your position early on the day. Wear the right clothes. At Murrayfield, in an open commentary position, for a Scotland v England rugby match, I wore pyjamas under my trousers to keep out the cold. They improved the commentary no end.

Commentary suffers from a lack of professional criticism. I do not remember, in forty-five years, reading a single intelligent analysis. Journalists tend not to understand the art, and those who do try become puzzled and annoyed by failure to master it. Inevitably standards fall when the mediocre becomes acceptable. Even within the BBC, and particularly in Local Radio, the quality of the commentaries has declined. It is perhaps no coincidence that the standard was highest under Lobby's leadership, soon after the war, when every word uttered was subject to friendly, but ruthless, scrutiny.

The qualities required by a top-class commentator defy close definition and perhaps this is why there are so few of them. Above all, it is necessary to have a sense of balance, but what does this mean? A feeling for the right word at the right time, an ability 'to strike the right note', an in-built sense of proportion and of timing, discretion and humour. In the stress of live broadcasting, words can trip you up. "It's a moment they will always forget", I said when the New Zealand team were presented to the Queen at Lords. "She's wearing dark black", was a comment made by Audrey Russell at a Royal Funeral. "If they keep up this pace", said a commentator on the Marathon Race at the Commonwealth Games, "the race should finish between twelve noon and mid-day"!

The voice that will hold the attention, not just for the couple of minutes of a news report, but

*'I wore pyjamas under my trousers to keep out the cold'*

for an hour or more, will be a voice 'with a smile in it', as one listener wrote, creating not excitement, which should speak for itself, but informed interest; a voice which compels attention by an attractive, but unmistakable, authority.

Ultimately, a perfect commentator must have total mastery of the technique of his job and a positive enthusiasm for the preparation, on which everything depends. In the next chapter I will recall the one man who had all of these virtues.

# CHAPTER 3

# The Master Broadcaster

As a broadcaster, there was nobody to touch him; it was like winning the Derby by twenty lengths. He spoke for the nation on State occasions, and his face, with the rise of television, was the best known in Britain.

Richard Dimbleby's early life had much in common with Churchill's. Neither shone at school, except at English; neither went to a university, but both had the capacity to illuminate events with an incomparable choice of words.

Richard Dimbleby was a large man, I prefer the word 'large' to 'fat'. His size led some people to think him pompous. Nothing could have been further from the truth; he was friendly and often very funny. Others called him sycophantic in his support of the Establishment and the Royal Family. In truth, all he did was to explain, on television, and describe, on the radio, what he saw in front of him. I think he took the view, as I certainly did, that if people wanted change they could vote for it.

Richard was a 'persona' – an acceptable person – rather than a 'personality' in the modern sense. Publicity came to him; he did not seek it. His astonishing appetite for work and his sheer ability meant that at times he seemed ever-present on either radio or television.

I came to know Richard only during

*Richard Dimbleby – master broadcaster.*

the last five years of his life from 1960 to 1965, when we often found ourselves covering the same event, Richard on television and myself on the radio. Our relationship was thus entirely professional; we met 'on the job' and discussed mutual problems. We were both doing the same thing, but in different ways. During all those five years he had cancer.

Even Richard could not be in two places at once and, now and again, I took his place as a television commentator on less important occasions such as the funeral of Dag Hammarskjöld, the UN Secretary-General, in Sweden, the NATO Tattoo at Arnhem and the visit of President Kennedy to the Vatican. Richard seemed, in a way, as insecure as anyone and just as anxious when somebody else took his place. He need not have worried. The BBC was as afraid of losing him as he apparently was of forfeiting his pre-eminent position; yet he was paid modest fees, never had a long-term contract, and was treated with niggling insensitivity over his expenses. However, he remained totally loyal to the BBC and the concept of public service broadcasting and, since his death in 1965, nobody has remotely challenged his primacy.

The world, of course, has changed since those days and broadcasting has changed with it. The probing interrogator, in interview or discussion programmes, is now the vogue.

Richard Dimbleby was a journalist; his father ran the family newspaper in Richmond, and Richard became the BBC's first News Reporter and later its first War Correspondent. What seemed to distinguish him from other journalists was his ability to 'change hats' from news reporter to set-piece commentator. Few journalists can do this today. They seem reluctant to accept that commentary is a separate art.

Before and after the War, Richard came under the influence of Seymour de Lotbinière, then Head of Outside Broadcasts, and his early radio commentaries showed that he had fully absorbed the essential basic technique as propagated by 'Lobby'. On turning to television, the up and coming medium, he adroitly made the change from description on the radio to 'annotation', as he put it, of a television picture.

When I took over the radio commentary of Trooping the Colour in 1961, the first thing I did was to listen to Richard's recordings.

Richard was very much more than a commentator. His fame blossomed with the rise of *Panorama* and he deftly handled the technical and human problems involved in presenting what was then the flagship of BBC Current Affairs. On radio, he was a much-loved voice on *Down Your Way*, a regular participant in *Twenty Questions*, and was in demand for countless other programmes.

Aspiring commentators of today might like to consider his attributes. He had an absolute mastery of commentary technique in both radio and television. He had a prodigious capacity for work and for preparation. His verbal fluency was complete – I never heard him say "er" – he would have thought it a waste of time! Above all he could always 'strike the right note' – that indefinable quality which marks out a great broadcaster.

In addition to all this, Richard had a splendid sense of humour and the ability to enthuse a team. Any producer will tell you that to have Richard as your main commentator was to halve the workload. You knew that whatever technical or other disaster might befall, he would get you through it somehow if it was possible. Even when the Royal Car was an hour late arriving at Tower Pier, after Princess Margaret's wedding in 1960, Richard and the producer, Antony Craxton, continued to hold the attention of viewers. "I was down to the last brick on the Tower of London", Richard said later.

In 1953, there were only two million television sets in the country; yet twenty-two million people gathered round them to watch the Coronation programme, produced by Peter Dimmock, and to hear Richard's impeccable commentary. That single event sold more television sets than anything else.

General Election nights also became a Dimbleby *tour de force* and still are, in the hands of his son David. With the producer's voice constantly in his ears and the latest results being dumped on his desk, he pulled the disparate strands of the programme together, making them a coherent whole – and for hours on end.

One of the first events on which Richard and I worked together was the Consecration of Coventry Cathedral in 1962. I had previously given the commentary on a film, made by John Laing, about the building of the Cathedral. I felt I knew a lot about it, but soon discovered that Richard knew more. His range of contacts and his ability to acquire facts quickly were quite remarkable and he was more than ready to share his knowledge. We had commentary boxes at the end of the nave and I had to climb through Richard's to get to mine above him. During the Service a lot of money, mostly pound notes (we had them then), spilled from the open collection plates onto the floor, causing a delay of about five minutes in the Service. Awkward – particularly for me on the radio. Luckily, my knowledge of the Cathedral saw me through. On the way down the ladder, I passed Richard with a broad grin on his face: "That was a bit tricky, wasn't it?" he said.

Richard was not so cheerful when, at the funeral of Pope John in Rome, Vatican Radio, through which lines were routed to the world, got into a slight muddle. Richard's television commentary ended up in Sweden and my commentary was taken by BBC Television as well as BBC Radio.

There were also problems with transmission on May 27th 1965, during the State Visit to Germany. It was a busy day for both of us in Berlin; I had broadcast live on the radio as the Queen addressed massed Berliners, and at 8.50 pm Richard was to introduce recorded highlights of the day on television. More technical trouble dogged his every word. Finally he was told that both sound and vision had been lost. "Jesus wept!" exclaimed Richard. Unfortunately, the microphone was very much alive.

At the end of that same State visit I accidentally dropped my microphone into the dock at Hamburg as 'Britannia' pulled away, so we were all square on disasters. Luckily my own remarks could not be recorded!

Richard Dimbleby and I were also together for the funeral of Sir Winston Churchill, which is described in Chapter 8 of this book. Richard's commentary position was next to mine in the West Gallery of St Paul's, and he had the monumental task of describing not only the procession to and from St Paul's but the Service as well. I remember offering him some supposed tit-bit of information, which I thought he might not know. "Oh yes", he said cheerfully, "I know that – and do *you* know..." and he gave me two alterations to the ceremonial in St Paul's.

That commentary, ending with the burial at Bladon, and all of it, except the Service, done from the monitor screen, was one of his finest. He had the rare ability to draw from any picture exactly what you wanted to know and to weave it together into an almost continuous commentary. Nobody complained that he talked too much. In television, it is not the quantity of talk which matters, but the quality.

We were both interested in commentary technique. Richard was not a sports broadcaster, although his bulk had been useful on occasion in the front row of the scrum at Mill Hill School. However, he was intrigued by the commentary problems and we often discussed them.

Richard enjoyed his fame. Sometimes, at rehearsals of big events, he would be consulted, as if he were the organiser. His large familiar figure was a magnet for attention. His Rolls Royce was perhaps a little ostentatious but who would begrudge it?

At no time did I guess at the extent of his cancer, or at the frequency of his radiotherapy treatment, following earlier surgery. How he got through his colossal workload is a mystery. He was a very courageous man and when he died in December 1965, aged fifty-two, I was honoured to be asked by the family to broadcast the radio commentary at his Memorial Service in Westminster Abbey on 4th January 1966. The thousands queueing outside were testimony to the bond of affection between him and the public. He was a man you could trust, a comfortable and comforting figure in a changing world.

Fifteen years later, a bust of Richard Dimbleby was unveiled in Poets' Corner. He was the first broadcaster to be so honoured.

Since Richard's death, others in broadcasting have been knighted, but one wonders if they will ever join him in Poets' Corner. He was the master.

# CHAPTER 4

# Test Match Special

Within seconds of 12.23, on an August day at Scarborough in 1955, Cyril Poole, a Nottinghamshire batsman of note, was wending his way to the wicket. At the end of his run stood Freddie Trueman of Yorkshire and England, a mop of black hair across his brow. Fred had taken wickets with his two previous deliveries. The 'hat-trick was on' and Cyril Poole was in no hurry to be part of it.

In the radio commentary box, I had been broadcasting since twelve noon on the North of England Home Service. On my right sat Bill Bowes, the former Yorkshire and England fast bowler; to my left was Arthur Wrigley, the doyen of cricket scorers. Propped against the window lay a stopwatch which, as Poole was taking his guard from the umpire, showed 12.24. Forty-five seconds remained before we would have to return our listeners to the studio, or be faded out. At 12.25 precisely, allowing fifteen seconds for a brief closing announcement and the switching of lines, the North of England would rejoin the National Home Service; there would be no leeway, no reprieve. Our admirable, if somewhat eccentric, announcer in Manchester, Roger Moffat, knew his duty; he had once curtailed a racing commentary two furlongs from the finish.

With twenty seconds left, Trueman ran in and bowled; Poole pushed forward and was caught at short leg. "It's a hat-trick!" I yelled into the microphone and, in the same breath, "back to the studio". It was my first, and only, hat-trick on the air and it had been achieved with seconds to spare.

That moment gave birth to *Test Match Special*, the ball-by-ball description of cricket Test Matches, which has become a national institution and the possible demise of which caused questions to be asked in the House of Commons.

At the time, I was the Senior Outside Broadcasts Producer in the North and had long felt that BBC cricket coverage, tied as it was to fixed periods, was vulnerable to the wayward nature of the game. In the regional broadcasting of those days, restriction was inevitable. Clearly, if a region 'opted out' of a certain programme, there was nothing I could do about that, but I did shudder at the thought of a Test Match, broadcast nationally, being faded out with a hat-trick or a century looming. What listeners wanted, I was sure, was continuous coverage, on a ball-by-ball basis, so that they could follow the entire match, as it developed, or dip in at any time for the latest score.

That autumn, in my Manchester office, I scrutinised the listening figures of the Home Service, Light Programme and 'Network Three', as it was then called. Listeners to the latter, a small but powerful body, were able to hear many hundreds of hours of music each year, but did so in such small numbers that at times they defied measurement. It occurred to me that the Controller of Network Three might appreciate some more listeners (he did) and that music lovers might not mind losing a tiny proportion of their staple diet (they did!).

Accordingly, I wrote a note to Charles Max-Muller, then Head of Outside Broadcasts, suggesting that continuous coverage of Test Matches might be provided on Network Three. Charles was no cricket fan, but he could see the merit of the idea. After a strenuous battle with the powers that be, and amid howls of protest from the music lobby, *Test Match Special* went on the air for the first time at Edgbaston in 1957, with Michael Tuke-Hastings as producer and the slogan "Don't miss a ball, we broadcast them all". And we have done ever since.

My own cricket education began back in 1926 when my father took me, aged six, to the Oval to see England play Australia. Jack Hobbs, dapper in his blue England cap, and Herbert Sutcliffe, capless with sleek, black hair, both made centuries and I saw the classic slow left-arm bowling of Wilfred Rhodes, playing in his last Test Match at the age of forty-eight. A year later, on 14th May 1927, came the first cricket commentary, given by Canon F. H. Gillingham on Essex vs New Zealand at Leyton. It was not a great success and was, appropriately, followed by the London Radio Dance Band playing *Don't Be Angry With Me*.

Between 1927 and 1934 there was no cricket commentary at all. Reports had to suffice. Teddy Wakelam, who was, in those early days, the acknowledged expert on the faster moving sports, had pronounced cricket as unsuitable for commentary. "Too slow", was his verdict, which was unfortunately accepted. How surprised he would have been by *Test Match Special!*

*Don Bradman in action with George Duckworth behind the stumps, 1930.*

My clearest recollection of that period is of Don Bradman making 254 against England at Lords in 1930. Years later I met Sir Don at a Test Match in Sydney. "That day", he told me, "I put the ball where I wanted it". You can say that again. His twinkling feet seemed to give him several options for the disposal of each ball delivered by Larwood, Tate, Allen, Geary and White – not an insignificant quintet of bowlers. Australia made 729 for six declared and I scored every run in my scorebook between swigs of lemonade from a bottle.

Later, in the thirties, Howard Marshall became the trail-blazer of cricket commentary, with his rich, mellow voice and ability to blend visual fact and personal impressions. He was at his best at the Oval in 1938 when Len Hutton made the then record Test Match score of 364 against Australia. It was a Timeless

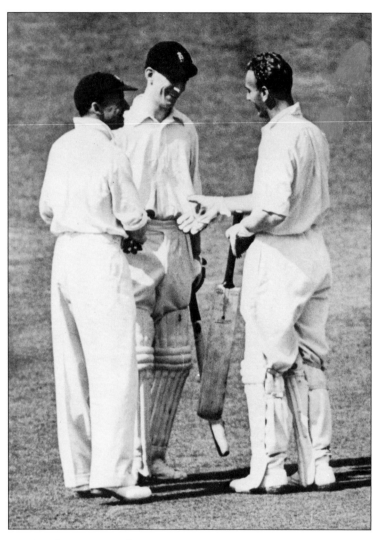

*Don Bradman congratulating Len Hutton, 1938.*

Test, which was just as well as Hutton batted for thirteen hours and twenty minutes. Poor Fleetwood-Smith, one of the Australian bowlers, took one wicket for 297 runs and wore such a hole with his front foot that Don Bradman, having a rare bowl, sprained his ankle and could not bat.

In the circumstances, Wally Hammond felt it safe to declare the innings closed at 903 for seven, Hedley Verity having hit the last ball before tea for four. One of the scoreboards ran out of figures and the '9' was put up in chalk. Bill Bowes, who was number eleven, told me years later that he had had visions of scoring the thousandth run. This might have been optimistic, as Bill took more wickets during his career than he made runs – an unusual feat.

During the war, spasmodic Inter-Services matches took place at Lords and elsewhere, culminating in the 'Victory Tests' of 1945. I remember hearing of these out in the Far East, where we were still engaged in fighting the Japanese, and feeling forgotten. Rex Alston was often the commentator on these war-time matches and had to be careful not to mention the weather for fear of helping the enemy. Even talk of a 'sticky' wicket might have given Hitler some useful hints. I saw one of these matches at Lords when on leave in London. A 'buzz-bomb' came chugging along and exploded on the far side of Finchley Road. Play was in progress at the time and the players deemed it wise to lie flat on the ground. After the bomb had gone off, Jack Robertson of Middlesex hit the next ball for six into the grandstand: the perfect way to cock a snook at the enemy.

Looking back, I calculate that two years of my life were spent talking about cricket on the air. It began at Lords in 1946 when I was asked to record a twenty-minute commentary on a County match as an audition. John Arlott was giving one of his first live broadcasts on the same match and, as I sat next to him listening to his then unfamiliar Hampshire burr, I felt I must stand a chance if the BBC had accepted such an extraordinary accent!

My first *Test Match Special* broadcast was in 1958 at Old Trafford. The match was England vs New Zealand. England won by an innings and 13 runs, with Peter May making 101. My fellow commentators were John Arlott and Freddie Brown, with expert comments by E. W. (Jim) Swanton and the New Zealand Test cricketer, W. E. Merritt.

A pattern of life in The Box soon emerged. Teamwork was of the essence. Egotism was out. It was the luck of the draw if your twenty-minute spell in each hour was exciting, and thus so much easier to broadcast, or dull with few runs scored and no wickets falling, when the skill of the commentator would be tested to the limit.

My own custom was to remain in the box throughout, watching each ball, even when not on the air. As a result I was very tired at the end of the day, but at least I knew exactly what had happened on the field and what had been said about it. The others would usually, and John Arlott always, leave the box after their spell at the microphone. Sometimes, a returning commentator, slipping into his place at the last minute, would raise a subject discussed in some detail a few moments before. He would be gently steered away from it. Poor Bill Frindall was anchored to his scoresheets throughout the day. The scorer records every run made, so he cannot leave the box until an interval in play – awkward sometimes!

It became clear from the letters which cascaded onto our desk each morning that a high proportion of our listeners were women. We seemed to lighten the day of many housewives, but also suffered the occasional rebuke. My description of an off-spinner bowling "with two short legs, one of them almost square" drew a sharp response from Basingstoke asking me to "kindly

*An off-spinner bowling 'with two short legs, one of them almost square'*

refrain from drawing attention to these infirmities". Somebody else said that Denis Compton "had been dropped when he was two". Out came the headed notepaper in defence of his mother!

Continuous broadcasting, for at least six hours a day, inevitably posed staffing problems. For regional county matches, one commentator could handle the three twenty-five minute spells usually involved. For ball-by-ball coverage, two more were needed, with an additional expert summariser and three engineers instead of one. A fresh approach would be welcome after twenty minutes of the same voice so, whatever other attributes they might have, the commentators would need to *sound* different. The best blend seemed to be one 'personality', one experienced broadcaster with his feet firmly on the ground, and one of our welcome visitors from overseas, to bring a new perspective to the game, as well as a different accent. What they all had to have in common was a mastery of commentary technique.

The commentators were supported by two former Test players, on duty for an hour at a time, to give their comments at the end of the over or at other convenient times. This format has remained largely unaltered, although in earlier days E. W. Swanton would give a masterly summing-up at the close of play.

When the different roles are understood and implemented the system works well. It falls apart if the commentator assumes the role of an expert, or if the real expert interrupts the commentary.

Over the years the 'personalities' have been John Arlott and Brian Johnston, while Rex Alston, myself in the sixties, and Christopher Martin-Jenkins in the more expansive period since the early seventies, did our best to restore order after one of their excursions up some exotic byway. Our overseas visitors included Alan McGilvray from Australia, who spoke so close to the microphone that he seemed in danger of swallowing it, Charles Fortune from South Africa and Tony Cozier from the West Indies. All excellent broadcasters and good friends.

Much of my early broadcasting was in fact on television with Brian Johnston. The atmosphere, as you may well appreciate, was light-hearted, especially when we were joined by Denis Compton. Messages would come into our ears from the control van, such as "Mention Trueman if you want a cup of tea" and we would answer on the air: "I think Fred Trueman should come on to bowl – he will need at least two slips". The result would be a cup of tea with two lumps of sugar!

On one occasion in 1949, I found myself sitting next to Prince Philip on the balcony at Lords, while I was on the air. It is difficult to bow with headphones on while holding a microphone. His amused smile seemed to accept my quick head-jerk as adequate obeisance.

A year later, Brian and I went up to Trent Bridge, Nottingham, for the first Test Match to be televised outside London. Our producer suggested that the umpires should be "slipped a quid" to come out five minutes late, due to a mistake in the billing in *Radio Times*. Needless to say they weren't, and didn't.

Much of the pleasure of broadcasting for *Test Match Special* has been to work with the eminent cricketers who have supplied expert comments. Trevor Bailey is the most experienced and most adept at putting his finger on the crucial tactical, or technical, point in a few words – and without cutting into the commentary. Jack Fingleton was most amusing in his blunt Australian style and I enjoyed working with Norman Yardley with whom I had a good rapport at the microphone. Fred Trueman has been a great success in more recent times, after some hesitation on my part in putting him on the air.

*Test Match Special* began in a fairly serious vein, sticking to the cricket and returning to the studio for music when it rained. I think this period saw John Arlott at his best. John was a poet and a wit at the microphone; his love of cricket was only one of his wide-ranging interests. He was also a lover of literature, pictures and wine, and was; of course, a writer of high repute. Genius can, however, be erratic and he had his off-days, when the cricket failed to engage his interest. He reacted well to the presence of distinguished visitors in the commentary box, producing a virtuoso performance for the visible audience. He did not, however, like his leg pulled on the air by Jack Fingleton, so we had to arrange the schedule to keep them apart.

I found John to be a surprisingly insecure man. He had no long-term contract with the BBC, yet he was the jewel in our crown. It was a strange situation which was rectified to some extent when I became Head of Outside

Broadcasts in 1969. Over lunch at the National Liberal Club, I told him he would never be dropped in my time and was answered by a relieved smile and another bottle of Beaujolais. Nobody should try to imitate John Arlott, because they will fail. He was a natural; he told me once that he rarely, if ever, listened to other people's commentaries.

"Are you John Arlott?" I was asked by a young boy during a match at Harrogate. Sadly, I shook my head. His freckled face retreated from the window of the commentary box to discuss this setback with other ten-year-olds. Eventually a grubby autograph book was thrust through the window. Flattered, Arthur Wrigley and I both signed. Handing the book back I suggested that its owner might swop the two signatures for one of John Arlott's. "Don't worry", said the enterprising lad, "we're going to".

In 1970, BBC Television decided on a change of policy. Frivolity was to take a back seat. In future, the commentaries would be given by former Test players who would stick strictly to the cricket. BBC Radio was the main beneficiary of this as I was quick to invite Brian Johnston, hitherto the almost exclusive property of television, to join the radio team.

The result for *Test Match Special* was dramatic. It was like switching from The Daily Telegraph to The Daily Mail; from the respected to the popular. It attracted new listeners, who had perhaps only a nodding acquaintance with cricket, but were intrigued by the non-stop mixture of description and reminiscence, especially when our team of raconteurs were told to keep talking when rain stopped play. On one occasion at least, Audience Research reported more listeners when there was no cricket. The match itself was becoming superfluous!

With John Arlott's quiet, subtle wit and Brian Johnston's gregarious personality, the atmosphere became positively jolly and, as with most good things, slightly 'over the top'. The programme attracted publicity from all quarters and the team was showered with gifts, particularly cakes, in such profusion that somebody also sent an antidote to tooth decay.

In 1973, I suggested an amalgamation of the Radio Outside Broadcasts and Sports News Departments. This was long overdue but my various predecessors had fought shy of a very difficult issue. Luckily, my previous experience as a

Personnel Manager in industry, and also as Head of Administration in the BBC North Region, had equipped me for the task and the fusion of the two departments was achieved to the benefit of the programmes and those involved in making them.

Cliff Morgan, the former will-o'-the-wisp Welsh fly-half, was installed as Sports Editor and Christopher Martin-Jenkins became Cricket Correspondent in succession to Brian Johnston, who had retired from the staff at the statutory age of sixty. Twenty years later he is still going strong! Last, but not least, Peter Baxter, at the age of twenty-six, was put in charge of the world-wide, round-the-year coverage that the proliferation of cricket and the success of *Test Match Special* had demanded. This reorganisation and the consequent appointments proved a great success and gave radio sport a new lease of life. I regard it as one of the most important things I did in the BBC.

In the fifties, much of my broadcasting was done in the North of England, and I described no less than twenty-one 'Roses' matches, the annual encounters between Yorkshire and Lancashire. One exciting game at Old Trafford in 1960 was building up to a climax in the extra half-hour on the last day. With *Children's Hour* due at five o'clock, we asked the Head of Programmes in Manchester if the cricket could continue until the match was over. He deliberated and came to a delicious compromise: "We will postpone *Children's Hour*," he said, "it will do the children more good to listen to the cricket". In the event, the children had their money's-worth, as Lancashire won off the last ball of the match.

In the sixties, Yorkshire had a great team, which won the County Championship seven times in ten years. This winning streak began at Hove in 1959, a match which I was lucky enough to broadcast. At lunch on the final day, Sussex were about 200 ahead with two wickets to fall. I was invited to lunch with the teams by Robin Marlar, the Sussex captain. Yorkshire were plainly hoping for a declaration, as there was to be a very early finish, but Marlar decided against it. It took Yorkshire some time to prise out the last two wickets and they were left 215 to win in about two hours. The first ball of the innings was hit over the sight-screen for six by Brian Stott. When Brian Close came in, he hit a ball into a nearby garden and three minutes were lost looking for it, but a fine innings by Doug Padgett and some lusty blows by Trueman saw Yorkshire home with a few minutes to spare. The Light Programme missed the end of the match, which was broadcast only to patients in local hospitals in Brighton and Hove. It can't have been good for their blood pressure.

Cricket is a game of infinite skill in which strength, subtlety, courage, humour, tactics and the weather all have their part to play. The matches tend to merge into each other as time passes, but I do recall clearly a wonderful innings by Ted Dexter against the West Indies at Lords and Colin Cowdrey coming into bat, with a broken arm, while Allen played out the last over for a draw. Other memories are of Trueman's three-hundredth Test wicket and some devastating bowling by Derek Underwood against Australia at the Oval in 1968.

In my mind's eye I see my ideal of a County match in the greenest part of this pleasant land. The opening bowler has the new ball in his hand. Play is about to begin. Cars are parked round the boundary, wives are pouring the morning coffee, the umpires are putting on the bails and the dogs are curling up under deck chairs. Six hours of bliss stretch ahead, as I raise my binoculars for the first ball. There is no finer way of wasting time and the people you meet are the most pleasant in the world. This is a far cry from today's cricket with its helmets, floodlights, white balls, limited overs, hospitality boxes and advertising logos.

During my time as Head of Outside Broadcasts, I did my best to ensure that cricket stayed on the air and was broadcast with skill, insight and humour. The commentary box at Lords, which was built, after much negotiation between myself and Gubby Allen and with his committee in 1974, will remain as my only tangible memorial, but I was pleased to receive a telegram when I retired, from Billy Griffith, the likeable and respected Secretary of the MCC (Marylebone Cricket Club), thanking me for "all I had done for cricket". I only hope that was true.

# CHAPTER 5
# State Opening

A hushed silence was supposed to descend on the House of Lords. The Queen sat impassively on the throne, the bewigged Judges huddled like learned sheep on the Woolsack, the Lords Spiritual shared the red leather benches with the exotic uniforms of ambassadors and diplomats, the Lords Temporal made a vivid splash of scarlet in the body of the Chamber and the tiaras of the Peeresses glinted in the television lights. All should have been quiet, but it wasn't.

A voice was ringing out loud and clear. It was giving a commentary, as 'Black Rod' made his way through the lobbies to summon the Commons. The voice was mine.

Newspapers avoid putting broadcasting on the front page unless something goes wrong with it and in this case it had.

It was 29th October 1974 and I was describing the State Opening of Parliament for the fifth time. As usual, the radio commentary box was high up above the Press and Public Galleries but, on this occasion, it had not been properly soundproofed. This was not the fault of the BBC, who had paid the Department of the Environment a substantial sum to erect and soundproof the box.

Lord Carrington complained about the noise and I was catapulted onto page one. Comment, however, was not all adverse. A member of the Royal Family was heard saying, "It was much more interesting with the commentary".

An anachronism is defined, in the *Oxford English Dictionary*, as 'any former thing, which is out of harmony with the present'. By this definition, the State Opening of Parliament may well be anachronistic. After all, one does not normally walk backwards or dress up like a Court playing card.

But would the alternative be preferable? A grey-suited President – and one wonders who that might be – would presumably arrive by car, instead of in the

Irish State Coach. He would walk briskly up the stairs to the House of Lords, if it still existed, and declare Parliament open. He would then return to wherever Presidents live. It is hard to imagine huge crowds, armed with Union Jacks and flasks of coffee, sleeping overnight on the pavements in order to witness this.

Pageantry needs spectators; otherwise it plays to an empty theatre. There is no point in a glittering procession through deserted streets. Our pageantry, based as it is on tradition, customs and symbolism, serves to remind us that we are part of a great nation. It is based on the monarchy and a thousand years of experience and precedent. Things must be seen to happen, whether it be a Coronation, a Royal Wedding or a Funeral. Just as in ancient times, when the King would arrive with ceremony and colour, in order to underline his importance, so it is today. The Royal Bodyguards were more necessary in days gone by, but they still survive, as do many of the ancient Offices of State.

There is no better example of our historical continuity than the State Opening of Parliament. State occasions are comparatively rare. The Opening of Parliament is the only annual one. Here we find all the essential ingredients which distinguish a State Occasion from, for example, a Royal Wedding.

State Occasions centre on the Monarch, who is always present unless prevented for some unavoidable reason. The ceremony is organised by the Earl Marshal of England and embellished by the compulsory presence of Garter King of Arms, the Heralds and the Pursuivants. The Royal Bodyguards, too, must be out in force. Ancient and mysterious titles are affixed to equally anonymous holders of them, but they all have a meaning etched in time. Few spectators will know who or what they are, but the sense of history is inescapable. Nothing happens without a reason and all who take part have a traditional role to fill. We have a genius for organising pageantry and have blended it with remarkable success into the modern world, with some inconvenience to traffic, perhaps, but nothing more.

From my lofty perch above the Press Gallery, I watch the Lords Spiritual and Temporal fill the five rows of inward-facing benches as well as the seats placed between them. It is quite a squash, with everyone talking at once. The scarlet robes of the Peers contrast with the elegant dresses of the Peeresses, the robes of the Bishops with the wigs of the Judges.

In due course, they will be joined by the Queen, who will send her Messenger, Black Rod, to summon the Commons. Then, the three Estates of Parliament will be present. In this modern age, so will radio, television and the press. The nation can see and hear the ceremony – and read about it in the papers.

The radio commentary is far from easy, not least because much of it has to be done from the television screen. With the naked eye, I can see only the House of Lords itself.

By now, the 'Regalia' will have arrived – with its own escort of Household Cavalry. The Comptroller of the Lord Chamberlain's office carries the Imperial State Crown, resplendent on a velvet cushion, into the Royal Gallery. Here he places it on a table and, for a few minutes, the nine hundred special guests standing on raised platforms on either side of the Gallery can have a good look at it.

The Queen and Prince Philip are on their way in the Irish State Coach, drawn by four Windsor greys and with a sparkling escort of Life Guards and Blues and Royals. By tradition, the Lord Chamberlain, Head of the Royal Household, stays behind to guard Buckingham Palace. A sort of 'hostage M.P.', supplied by the Commons, keeps him company. One can't be too careful.

In medieval times, the 'Chamber' was where the King kept the Royal Jewels, money and important documents. The chief officer was called 'Master Chamberlain', hence the present title, not to be confused with the Lord *Great* Chamberlain, whose role is now purely ceremonial.

The BBC has placed a commentator outside the Palace and another on the roof of the Henry VII Chapel of the Abbey, to describe the arrival at Westminster.

A tricky moment for all concerned. For the coachman guiding his horses through the narrow arch, for the band timing the National Anthem to coincide with the exact moment of arrival, for the BBC engineers switching the acoustic background from outside to inside. The cue for this is a trumpet call as the coach swings round to negotiate the arch and as the Royal Standard is raised on the Victoria Tower.

It is also my cue to pick up the commentary.

The Queen and Prince Philip are met at the Royal Entrance by the Earl

Marshal (the Duke of Norfolk) and by the Lord Great Chamberlain (Lord Cholmondeley – pronounced Chumley), who carries the gold key of the Palace of Westminster at his waist. Both these titles existed in Tudor times and were then held by two of the seven 'Great Officers of State', who effectively ran the country under the crown.

Nowadays their role is largely ceremonial, although the Earl Marshal, as Head of the College of Arms, has total responsibility for State Occasions. Not so long ago, they were required to walk backwards up the Royal Staircase: a difficult, possibly dangerous and somewhat ludicrous practice, which has sensibly been stopped.

They intend no slight on the Queen as they now turn about and the whole Royal Procession moves up the twenty-six steps leading to the Robing Room, the Royal Gallery, the Prince's Chamber and the House of Lords.

The scene is like some baronial castle come to life. On either side of the staircase stand Troopers of the Household Cavalry; Life Guards on the right, Blues and Royals on the left. They were on opposite sides in the Civil War of 1642 as well. There is a gentle gleam of breastplates and helmets, a glint of drawn swords and a rustle of dresses and uniforms as the procession makes its way up the stairs. At the top, it takes up its position in the Royal Gallery. We will examine its composition more closely in a moment.

Meanwhile, the Queen and Prince Philip turn right into the Robing Room.

They disappear from my television picture, as no camera watches the Queen put on the Imperial State Crown and the long, crimson Robe of State. I have no personal experience, but I understand the crown is heavy and it is necessary to keep the head still. The train of the Robe of State is carried by four Pages of Honour in scarlet coats.

While the Queen is getting ready – a long mirror is provided – let us look at the fairy-tale procession which awaits her outside.

Broadly speaking, it consists of Officers of the College of Arms, Great Officers of State, holders of ancient Parliamentary Offices and members of the Royal Household. It is living history.

First come the Heralds and Pursuivants in their sleeveless coats of scarlet and gold, called tabards. They are worn only in the presence of the sovereign and are embroidered with the Royal Arms. In the 14th century, they were announcers and scorekeepers at the great tournaments of those days. They would go ahead to say the King was coming. Symbolically they do the same today. To do their job, they had to recognise Coats of Arms at the tournaments. This has led to their modern expertise in genealogy as officers of the College of Arms, and members of the Royal Household.

The Pursuivants, junior to the Heralds, have beguiling names like Rouge Croix and Bluemantle. Occasionally one blows his nose to prove he is real.

Behind walk the Heralds: Somerset with York, Lancaster with Norfolk, Richmond with Windsor. Then come the Kings of Arms. The 'Pack of Cards' is almost complete.

Next, on the rich blue carpet which covers the length of the Gallery, come three 'Great Officers of State', whose titles have survived to the present day. The Lord Privy Seal and the Lord President of the Council walk together. Behind them, in a black velvet Court Suit, a Robe of Damask, trimmed with gold, and wearing a full-bottomed wig, comes the Lord Chancellor. He is the highest civil subject in the land, and the holder of the most historic and dignified office under the Crown. Centuries ago he would be found, with his educated staff of clerics, behind a 'cancella', or screen, put up in the Great Hall to give them privacy as they issued the King's orders. Hence the 'Lord Chancellor'.

May we return for a moment to the humble broadcaster?

Unable to see the procession with the naked eye, and temporarily lacking a television picture of it, he relies on his carefully arranged notes and the immaculate timing which, at 11.27 precisely, will cause the Lord Great Chamberlain to raise his white wand as a signal for the doors of the Robing Room to be opened. On either side stand State Trumpeters who sound a fanfare, as the Queen is seen framed in the doorway. Appropriately, the microphones relaying the fanfare are cradled in the arms of Elizabeth I and Henry V, whose statues flank the doorway. The television picture now returns, after its short excursion by film round the Palace of Westminster, and I can see this tide of history moving up the length of the Royal Gallery. The Queen, in a long golden dress, wears the Imperial State Crown containing over three thousand diamonds, pearls, sapphires, emeralds and rubies, including the great

Second Star of Africa. She raises her left arm and takes Prince Philip's hand. Immediately in front of her, symbolising her authority as Head of State and Head of the Church of England, are carried the Sword of State, which proved too heavy for Field Marshal Montgomery in his declining years, and the rather lighter Cap of Maintenance.

Then, walking backwards – safe enough on the flat – come the Earl Marshal, carrying his ebony staff, and the Lord Great Chamberlain with his white wand. Navigation, so he told me, is by means of squinting down at the black shoes of the Yeomen of the Guard who line the Royal Gallery, and taking care to avoid their banner, which is lowered in salute as the Queen approaches. They were created by Henry VII after the Battle of Bosworth in 1485 and are the oldest of the Royal Bodyguards. They wear their traditional Tudor uniforms of scarlet and gold, and round black hats. Earlier in the day, they will have searched the vaults for any modern Guy Fawkes.

In front of them walk two important and resplendent figures. Black Rod, the Queen's Messenger, in black Court Dress, will shortly be despatched to fetch the Commons. He is a distinguished officer of high rank. Walking with him is Garter King of Arms, his velvet tabard smothered in scarlet and gold, with the Royal Arms embroidered on the back, front and both sleeves. Truly the King of Hearts.

Finally, behind the Queen walks an assortment of Lords, Ladies and Gentlemen of high and distinguished rank holding, usually temporarily, a variety of mysterious titles such as 'Woman of the Bedchamber', and 'Gold Stick in Waiting', who must be glad that he is no longer required to sleep outside the royal bedroom.

Scarlet, gold and white predominate in this river of elegance and historic pageantry as it flows – and that somehow is the right word – slowly through the Royal Gallery to the Prince's Chamber. Exercising their right to be the 'Nearest Guard', the impressive figures of the Corps of Gentlemen at Arms bring a splash of colour to the oak-panelled walls. They wear scarlet uniforms with gold epaulettes and from their silver helmets protrude white swans' feathers. They are all distinguished ex-officers. "A sumptuous troop of Gentlemen" Henry VIII called them in 1509, and he was right.

It is 11.29. My eyes are fixed on the doorway leading into the House of Lords. The lights are dimmed. Everyone rises; the lights go up, and there is the Queen, the ultimate source of honour and constitutional power, who reigns but does not rule. It is a magnificent piece of theatre.

The Robe of State is draped carefully by the pages down the four red-carpeted steps leading up to the throne – the Chair of State – the Seat of Majesty but not of Power. Prince Philip sits (slightly lower) to the Queen's left. Our gold microphones peep coyly from the figure of an angel next to the throne to pick up the Queen's voice. She waits until everyone is in position; the pages and

ladies-in-waiting on either side, the Sword of State and the Cap of Maintenance held two steps below the throne. I stop my commentary. It is 11.30 exactly.

"My Lords, Pray be seated."

The supremacy of the Monarchy has been subtly demonstrated. The House of Lords at this moment becomes the 'Parliament Chamber'. The Lord Great Chamberlain raises his wand and Black Rod sets off through the corridors and lobbies to summon the Commons, leaving behind him a scene frozen like some coloured waxwork tableau.

Black Rod has about a hundred yards to go, preceded by a mobile television camera. My radio commentary is given from the television screen. Ahead of Black Rod marches the Superintendent of Custodians, in a dark blue uniform and peaked cap. At intervals he shouts, "Hats off, strangers". Having checked with him in advance the exact points at which he will do this, I am able to pause as his voice rings out.

Then, symbolising their right to be independent, the doors of the Commons are slammed with a resounding bang in Black Rod's face. Equally satisfying for our sound effects are the three loud knocks which he makes with his ebony staff.

The doors are opened. "Black Rod!" is the cry from the Doorkeeper. At this moment, the Queen can see the Speaker, exactly opposite to her, but 141 yards and two feet away. That is about as close as she will ever get, as the Monarch may not enter the Commons. Charles I saw to that by trying to arrest the five members in 1642. A painting in the Peers' Corridor reminds us of the fact.

Now I describe Black Rod bowing to either side, as he advances to the table of the House, on which our microphones are placed. He bows a third time: "Mr Speaker, the Queen commands this honourable House to attend Her Majesty immediately in the House of Peers".

The Members of Parliament come, two by two, noisily and quite slowly. In front are the Prime Minister and the Leader of the Opposition, in apparent amity. Behind them, the two hundred members who have tickets. There is not room for more and they will have to stand anyway. Eventually the third Estate of

Left: *State Opening of Parliament. The view from the commentary box.*

Parliament is assembled behind the Bar of the House of Lords and I contrast their rather drab lounge suits with the dazzling colour in front of them. But they have the power.

Now the Lord Chancellor mounts the four steps and hands 'The Gracious Speech from the Throne' to the Queen who, wearing spectacles nowadays, reads it, in a clear voice, and without a single 'fluff', as we call it in the business.

The Queen is an experienced broadcaster, who puts many a professional to shame. The speech is, of course, written by the Government of the day and does not necessarily represent the Queen's own views. It is as close as the Monarchy gets to party politics.

The Speech usually lasts about ten minutes. Then, quite quickly, the regal tableau dissolves and the colour fades. The rich robes, dazzling uniforms and shimmering dresses, the sparkling jewels and ancient titles fade away.

The men in lounge suits go back to the Commons to run the country.

> "Her Majesty Queen Elizabeth, thus being conducted with Royalty into the Upper House of Parliament and apparelled in her Parliament Robes, there she sat, in princely and seemly sort, under a high and rich canopy, the Lords Spiritual and Temporal before her, ranged in order due – and the Judges on the Woolsacks in the midst."

Sounds familiar? It was written in 1571.

So, is the State Opening of Parliament an anachronism? Those who hold that view would argue that it is an expensive waste of time, which disrupts the traffic. In fact, most of those involved are either members of the Government or part-time and unpaid participants in a great occasion. The soldiers, coaches and uniforms are, in the main, there anyway. Hard currency from tourism will help to balance the books. The State Opening does not take place in the rush hour, so traffic disruption is reduced, although it exists.

The Monarchy fosters our sense of nationhood. In tribal terms, it is about chieftainship and the need from time to time to see the tribal chiefs assembled in one place; in this case the House of Lords. The State Opening also serves to explain the role of the Monarch as Head of State, under the 'umbrella' of which we can change our elected Government, where the real power lies, in three weeks flat – a fact which never ceases to amaze Americans.

On Tuesdays the Queen grants an audience to the Prime Minister of the day. She has the constitutional right to be consulted, to encourage and to warn. It must seem to the Queen that Prime Ministers, like policemen, get younger all the time. What passes between them is never divulged, but access to the advice of the most experienced Head of State in the world must be of great value to a young PM.

We belong to schools, churches and societies. We work for companies and firms. We like to see them flourish. In the same way we take pride in our nation if it is admired and feel shame if it is not.

State and Royal Occasions provide rare opportunities for displays of national unity. They preserve our history and our heritage in an unique manner. They provide a focus for our loyalty and convey a feeling of belonging to something respected and of which we are proud.

Our pageantry stems from the oldest hereditary Monarchy in the world. Nowhere is it carried out with such elegant and tasteful precision. Nowhere does it run so exactly to time. As a broadcaster in many countries I can say that with some feeling.

Lord Cobbold, a former Lord Chamberlain, is quoted as saying, "All Ceremonial is ridiculous, unless it is perfect". How true and how fortunate that British pageantry is the finest in the world. But then we have had a thousand years of experience.

# CHAPTER 6
# Round the World with the Queen

It hit the deck with a splintering crash, close to the Queen's left foot. A stain appeared on the white wood; medium dry in colour. Freddie Reed had dropped his glass of sherry.

The Royal Yacht, Britannia, was anchored in Auckland harbour and assorted media representatives, who were to report the Royal Tour of New Zealand, were gathered on deck for a cocktail party. It was 1963.

The royal dustpan appeared as if by magic, followed by the royal mop. Order was restored and, in a generous gesture, Freddie, a star photographer, was given another glass of sherry, presumably to have a shot at the other foot.

Later that same evening, he was stationed on the steps of the St James Theatre to take the Queen's picture as she arrived for an opera performance. Using all his professional expertise, Freddie pressed the camera button - and the flashbulb exploded.

For the second time on the same evening the Queen found herself surrounded by broken glass. She paused on the steps. The collective breath was held. Was Freddie to be sent to the Tower? "Mr Reed," said the Queen, "this just isn't your day".

Freddie's contribution to the welfare of the Press Party was considerable. At the first press briefing, he would make a point of complaining about almost everything. Popular targets were the lack of an open vehicle for cameramen in front of the royal car, the ludicrous positioning of the press bus, at the rear of the motorcade, the 'pool' system restricting access to certain events and, most importantly, the opening hours of the hotel bar.

It was rare for Freddie not to get all of these matters put right. We were duly grateful. Coverage of the tour and the morale of the press party both improved.

We would have gathered, a week or so earlier, in a downstairs room at Buckingham Palace, to meet the senior members of the Royal Household who would be accompanying the Queen and Prince Philip. We would be greeted by the Private Secretary, Press Secretary, Ladies-in-Waiting and Equerries. In some magical way, they seemed to know all about us.

For once, we would be properly dressed. Legendary journalists like René MacColl of the *Daily Express*, Vincent Mulchrone of the *Daily Mail* and Leslie Thomas, later to become a best-selling author, would appear in immaculate suits. The ladies, among them Anne Sharpley of the *Evening Standard*, and the BBC's Audrey Russell, would be in their finery .

How different it would soon be. Festooned with tape recorders, cameras and typewriters, we would sweat our way round the world, dressed solely for practical convenience.

In hot countries I wore long, specially-made bush shirts equipped with extra pockets for spare batteries, stopwatches, guide books; ham sandwiches and a tie to be put on for important interviews and taken off again immediately afterwards; the badge of respectability.

On my first overseas trip for the BBC, to Nigeria in 1960, I allowed the tailor to equip me, in my innocence, with a pith helmet, shorts and a cummerbund, narrowly avoiding being the laughing stock of the press party. Luckily, the penny dropped in time and all were discarded .

The Queen and Prince Philip were more interested in our coverage plans than I had expected. In Quebec in 1964, it was my turn, in a long line, to be presented. Prince Philip, standing next to the Queen, quizzed me about BBC radio plans. "Daily news coverage, Sir, some live outside broadcasts and a weekly half-hour programme". What interested me was that the Queen held up the presentation line to listen to my answer.

In the sixties, as a Staff Commentator, I covered five major Royal Tours to Commonwealth countries, as well as State Visits to Germany, Ethiopia, the Sudan and Persia. There was also a brisk trade in Independence ceremonies and I described the Union Jack being hauled down in Kenya, Nigeria, Zanzibar and Tanganyika (now Tanzania).

I was lucky to have such experienced companions as Godfrey Talbot and Audrey Russell on many occasions. In New Zealand, Australia and Ethiopia, John Timpson and TV cameraman Bernard Hesketh were congenial colleagues.

The size of the BBC, with its multiplicity of outlets, made life complicated for a small radio team relying almost entirely on the often meagre technical resources of our hosts. Only rarely was a BBC engineer with us; television, with its heavier equipment, at least had a cameraman and sound recordist in addition to a reporter and producer.

Our primary duty in radio was to service the news bulletins. Godfrey Talbot would think nothing of broadcasting a dozen dispatches in a day. We covered big events 'live', both for the BBC and for our host country, who made good use of our services. Independence Ceremonies, Openings of Parliament, Arrivals, Departures and the Queen's first public speech to the citizens of Germany in Berlin in 1965, spring to mind.

Our main regular programme was an amalgam of the week's events to which we all contributed and the tapes of which were sent by air to ensure good technical quality. Airline timetables are engraved on my heart. So is the Home Service programme which I rescued from the air freight office at Teheran Airport, and hurled personally onto a British Airways flight as the doors were closing. It contained, among other things, a description of the State Banquet given by the

Queen Elizabeth in Bonn, State Visit to Germany, 20th May 1965.

Shah of Persia and Queen Soraya, the lavishness of which took one's breath away when compared with the poverty and rutted roads outside.

The World Service, as we were uneasily aware, broadcast twenty-four hours a day – 'Round the World Round the Clock'. This could catch you out even when asleep.

"We are rolling," said the voice at 2.45 am on the telephone in Canada, implying that a recording machine was running at that moment. "Rolling what?" I replied sleepily. "Didn't you get the cable?" said the voice from Bush House in London, (I had not) "We need one minute for the 3.00 am bulletin on tomorrow's Royal Programme". Heaving myself out of bed, I scribbled some notes on the back of an envelope, had a quick rehearsal with my stopwatch, and delivered sixty seconds (exactly) down the telephone. Minutes later it came back to me on my bedside radio. I turned over and went to sleep. A strange world.

We were working tourists. If the Queen worked fifteen hours, we worked eighteen. "Did you travel on the Britannia?" I am often asked. No, we did not, nor on the royal plane. The BBC booked our long-distance flights and the host nation would supply press planes and buses within their own country.

The 'writing press' can cable stories and pictures to meet deadlines from the Press Centre, but broadcasting is different; it requires special facilities and never finally 'goes to press'. We need access to local studios for radio telephone circuits to London, planned and booked in advance. These studios are often off the route, so special transport is needed.

With three in the radio team, one will normally be ahead at the next port of call, one always with the Queen and the third gathering background material and seeing that our tapes reach home. We set out with a master plan and decide the daily details over breakfast.

Arrivals are important; they make the news. A new Royal Tour or State Visit has begun. There is speculation in the air. Will this or that country remain in the Commonwealth? How will our old enemies, the Germans, greet the Queen? All this is good stuff and the press are happy; their stories and pictures hit the front pages. Thereafter their faces grow longer and the cables from their editors are less enthusiastic. The BBC presses doggedly on, reporting what actually happens, but also capturing the sights, sounds and voices of the country concerned. But one must be honest: it is the things that go wrong that make the news; the omitted curtsey, complete with picture, the slipping gangplank, the incautious word: they will be the headlines, as will an arm round the royal waist or an over-zealous reporter from overseas. The Queen does not give interviews. The British press know the form.

Long voyages by Britannia do not appeal to the Queen, so it is despatched ahead in its noiseless splendour with its soft-shoed crew and air of calm efficiency; loaded no doubt with Malvern water and China tea, in addition to all the food and drink required for the receptions and dinners on board. It becomes a sort of floating Palace and a necessary haven, as well as a working office, for the Queen and Prince Philip. They will follow by air.

So let us look at a typical day, but scatter the fifteen or so Royal engagements, the four speeches and three changes of clothes, around the world. I went to thirty-one countries with the Queen in the sixties, so let me try to capture the flavour of some of them; at the same time keeping an eye on the BBC.

We start at Cologne in 1965. The royal plane is due for the first State Visit to Germany since the war. I am describing the arrival 'live' for the BBC Home Service. Next to me is a German commentator. He wants to know what the Queen will be wearing. I can help him there, as I have the details supplied by Buckingham Palace: a green two-piece suit. He is grateful. The aeroplane taxies to a halt – and the Queen gets out in yellow. Apparently, the royal party, en route to Cologne, was told that the German Guard of Honour was in bottle-green uniforms. Result – a quick change of costume. Good thinking – but I got an odd look from my German colleague.

Sometimes, the Queen and Prince Philip would come ashore by launch from Britannia, as at St John's, Antigua, in the West Indies. I had agreed to help the local radio station with the commentary. My Antiguan co-commentator started the broadcast but, almost at once, handed the microphone to me. He then departed, with his camera, to take pictures for the family album, which apparently took priority. Not knowing the length of the programme, I struggled gamely on until not only the Queen, but also the press bus with my lunch in it, had disappeared in a cloud of dust. It felt like describing my own funeral.

In Fiji, the first thing the Queen has to do is to drink a rather unpleasant concoction out of a coconut shell. This sign of friendship tastes like toothpaste. Having survived the ordeal in 1963, she was warmly received in the streets of

Suva, the capital. At least, that is what I cabled to London. A press colleague demurred: lukewarm at best, was his view. He switched on his radio. My own words, read by the announcer but not attributed to me, were in the World Service news headlines. "Oh well," he said, "you must be right" – and put them into his own dispatch.

So the Queen and Prince Philip have arrived. The Guard of Honour has presented arms; thousands line the streets. A civic reception is next on the agenda.

In Karachi in 1961, we had to hire a taxi whose driver, in an excess of illegal zeal, inserted his battered vehicle immediately behind the royal Rolls Royce and in front of the High Commissioner's. The Queen and Prince Philip, sitting on the folded roof with their feet on the back seat, were greeted with great enthusiasm, but the biggest cheers were reserved for the unexpected comic turn following behind until, sadly, the police stopped the fun and ushered us down a side street.

Civic pride takes different forms. In Stuttgart, a patch of rather off-colour grass was painted green. In New York in 1976, the red carpet was laid by Marines exactly one minute before the Royal Launch reached the landing stage; thirty seconds later, after the Queen and Prince Philip had walked on it, it was promptly removed. I believe that is called time and motion study.

In Wall Street, the crowds were enormous and, in my view, dangerous; hemmed into a narrow street and unable to retreat even if they wished. Near me the cameramen of CBS, ABC and NBC – that highly competitive trio – were having a private battle for filming positions. The police had obviously misjudged the warmth of the welcome. In these situations, the Queen is at her best. She displayed no trace of alarm as a narrow passageway fortunately opened up in the crowd, held back by police, Royal Household and the press, to take her to the safety of the end of the street.

It is still only mid-morning on this specimen day. The Queen and Prince Philip may have separate engagements or they may be together for the opening of a Commonwealth Parliament.

It is modelled on Westminster lines, protocol anxiously observed, white gloves *de rigueur* for the ladies, and children, eyes popping out with excitement, waving flags in the street outside. It may mean a live broadcast for me; more probably we send recordings.

In New York, the morning is more relaxed. The Queen is to visit Bloomingdales department store and I am with the crowds outside on the pavement with my recording machine. Americans have, I suspect, a secret longing for a Royal Family and are avid followers of ours. But they stick up for their President as well, so that the BBC doesn't get the wrong idea. I interview a group of rather precocious children who have been modelling Bloomingdales' latest creations. What do they think of the Queen?

"A very lovely lady," is the unanimous verdict.

Also, luckily, a lady of stamina. There are two more engagements before lunch and now, in our worldwide morning, the Queen is in Calcutta. A museum looms ahead and the heart sinks a little. A link-up with London is due soon and this is unlikely to yield much. Some fossils, in a glass case, are being explained to the Queen, whose feet are killing her. With great dexterity, she removes each foot in turn from its shoe, wiggles her toes and replaces the foot without knocking over the shoe or allowing her expression of interested attention to falter. Ten out of ten.

In Pakistan, a morning is spent driving from Peshawar up the Khyber Pass. Near the fort of Landi Kotal which guards the top of it, the Queen and Prince Philip stand a few feet from the border with Afghanistan, marked by white stones. Some yards away, on the other side, the Afghan Border Guard, smartly turned out, presents arms to Royal visitors to another country. With the rugged hills as a backcloth, it is a strange and unforgettable scene.

As we jump around the world, let us call in now at Government House, St Vincent, for an Investiture. It is 1966. Most of the hardbitten press don't bother to go and are already propping up the bar. The 'good and great' of this little West Indian island are assembled in an elegant drawing room. Faces beam from beneath new hats. A distinguished-looking man kneels and is tapped on each shoulder with a sword. The Queen then shakes his hand and they talk for a few moments. About six other decorations are given. Pride is at bursting point all round. In my view, the transition from Empire to Commonwealth has been one of the wonders of the twentieth century. But, sadly, in many cases 'instant democracy' has not worked.

Lunch takes unexpected forms. Usually just a sandwich but, in St Kitts, a four-course meal was served (backwards) by the local domestic science class, to the bemused press corps. We started with coffee, which happened to be ready, and worked our way through the pudding towards the main course. The young cooks had logistical problems but so did we. René MacColl made a graceful speech of thanks for this unusual repast and we fled to what turned out to be a very slow boat. This was to take us to the sister island of Nevis, where Admiral Nelson was married. To the great amusement of Prince Philip, the entire British press arrived long after the Royal Party.

Children's rallies are popular in the afternoons. Quite often the children are lined up to spell the Queen's name. It was so on a sports field in Pakistan. Unfortunately, they spelled ' E L Z I A B E T H ' and the file of children representing the 'I' was being chased into the right place by a frantic teacher, just as the Queen reached the Royal Box. Prince Philip, if I remember rightly, took temporary refuge behind a nearby aspidistra. Both he and the Queen are adept at keeping a straight face to avoid any embarrassment; this must be difficult when, as has happened, a rather overweight lady completes her royal curtsy by falling on her bottom.

Let us move on to a carnival in St Lucia. I am helping the local radio station with the commentary. Most of the Press are back in the hotel listening, with half an ear, to my commentary in case any news emerges. One of the carnival floats tips over and collapses about ten yards from the Queen. Nobody is hurt and the Queen is in no danger but, as if by magic, the press materialise, notebooks at the ready. Could I make it five yards? No, I couldn't. 'Queen startled'? She never turned a hair. Grumbling at my lack of co-operation, they go off to 'file' (the jargon) their stories. "Float just misses Queen" is the best headline they can muster – but at least it is on the front page.

So the Royal motorcade drives on. We are in Africa now and it is nearing teatime. The entire population of every little village is out in force. Banners are strung across the road. 'Goodbye. Come again' says one, as we enter. 'Welcome Elizabeth', as we leave. But nobody minds. Banners can be misleading. On Prince Edward Island in Canada, 'Welcome to Charlottetown' conveyed a different message when the initial 'C' fell off!

Now it is late afternoon and a garden party in the grounds of Government House; many guests are presented before the Queen gets a cup of tea. Early evening and, by magic carpet, we are in Addis Ababa. Emperor Haile Selassie of Ethiopia is presenting a horse to the Queen. They are both small and the horse is large. They stand one on either side of its tossing neck. The Emperor bobs up and down making a little speech. Eventually the Queen is one horse to the good.

Unexpectedly, the entire press corps is invited to the State Banquet. It is the only one I have eaten anywhere in the world, although I have reported many. Suits and dresses are unpacked hurriedly and made to look tolerably respectable. The Queen looks magnificent and makes her fourth speech of the day. Now only a firework display stands between her and some well-earned sleep. Tomorrow it will start all over again.


An analogy with the theatre may be appropriate.

The Queen and Prince Philip are, of course, the stars of the show, constantly in the spotlight. 'Speaking parts' are played by the Head of State of the host country and his wife or her husband. The Royal Household have 'walk-on' parts only, but have planned the whole production with meticulous care many months before. Every inch of every route has been measured and scrutinised, every crumb of every meal approved. Lists of those to be presented have been agreed, 'photo opportunities' arranged for press and TV. Office staff, footmen and the indispensable hairdresser will be on board Britannia, clothes for each day carefully chosen, presents for their hosts labelled and ready.

What is less certain is the size of the audience. It has varied, in my experience, from millions in Calcutta, swarming up trees, hanging out of windows and jamming the pavements, to the streets of Quebec, quite empty for fear of French-Separatist trouble and lined by police and soldiers with nobody to control.

I recall the evening light in the 'pink city' of Jaipur with the Queen riding on an elephant with the Maharajah, into the City Palace. "Fasten seat belts!" shouted Prince Philip from the elephant behind. The streets were packed. The only means of reaching the broadcasting studio was by that useful taxi, a bicycle rickshaw. A handful of rupees did the trick and, bell ringing, we hurtled along, scattering people in all directions. The driver never had so much fun in his life. Triumphantly, I reached the microphone ready to record my piece. "You are one minute late," said the voice from London.

So finally, in our theatrical analogy, what of the Press Party in their role of critics and photographers of the production? Most of us would agree that Royal

Tours are exhausting fun. In hot countries, perspiration and inspiration unfortunately don't go hand in hand. Sometimes the cumulative effect of packing, travelling, getting shirts washed, changing currency and paying bills leaves little time for broadcasting's vital preparation. Four or five hours' sleep would be par for the course. On one occasion I had to look on the back of my bedroom door, not to check the price of the room, but to remind myself where I was. It was St Lucia, a pleasant island, full of bananas.

For the Queen, with the constant support of Prince Philip, one has nothing but admiration. Only impeccable staff work, superb briefing, total relief from 'tourist' chores and a good night's sleep could possibly produce such a relaxed attitude each morning and throughout the long day ahead. The hands to be shaken, speeches made, factories visited, medals bestowed and clothes changed must seem daunting tasks at the start of the day.

Luckily the Queen seems physically strong. With age, though, she will not be able to do so much and younger members of the Royal Family will have to play a bigger part. Prince Charles and, notably, Princess Anne do this.

In my experience, Royal Tours and State Visits give pleasure to many and, particularly to the poor and to children, they bring a few moments of fairytale magic. Look into the faces of villagers in India or Africa and you will see not envy, but joy and wonder. Why is it that the most cynical pressman is first in the queue to be presented to the Queen? Why is our Royal Family so fully reported in the foreign press? The mystique of our Monarchy acts like a magnet. Republicanism within the Commonwealth may well increase; even in Britain the role of the Monarchy is questioned by some. This is understandable in a world of changing alliances.

As Prince Philip himself told the Canadians, "The Monarchy exists, not for its own benefit, but for that of the country...if people don't like it, they should change it".

How many would willingly take on a job of service, with no retirement age, no moment free from responsibility as Head of State and no holiday of your choice? Yet that is exactly what the Queen has done for over forty years.

# CHAPTER 7
# Over to Twickenham

The referee was looking at his watch. The Scottish team were thinking of the pints of shandy awaiting them in the dressing room. Andy Hancock was feeling neglected on the England left wing.

It was the Calcutta Cup rugby match at Twickenham in 1965 and, at the end of a rather dull game, Scotland were leading 3 – 0. Up in the commentary box in the West Stand, my stop-watch showed that time was up.

Suddenly, Hancock received the ball from Mike Weston close to his own goal line. It was only his third pass in the match and he had dropped the other two. He was about to make amends in style.

Surprised, not only at getting the ball, but also at holding on to it, he set off without delay for the other end of the ground. He had about a hundred yards to go. It was in his favour that his opposite number, the Scottish right wing, lay buried in the scrum and was thus not available to tackle him. Also, the Scottish back row were slow to come across and, as a result, Hancock found himself almost in the clear and approaching the half-way line.

Two threats remained. The first was posed by Ian Laughland, a centre threequarter, who was beaten by an inward and outward swerve. Now only Stewart Wilson, the full back, stood between Andy and his hour of glory. Distracted by Budge Rogers following up on the inside, Wilson slipped slightly and missed the tackle. Andy Hancock, although perilously close to the touchline, had a clear run and thirty yards to go.

On the recording of my commentary, replayed regularly in nostalgic programmes and on cassettes, I say, "Hancock is going to score the most amazing try for England – and he scores NOW!" – the yell of "NOW!" coincides with his dive over the line by the corner flag. He might have run round behind the posts to make the conversion easier, but after such a marathon effort, settled for what he got. Don Rutherford missed the kick and the match was drawn 3 – 3. In those days, a try was three points; today, England would have won 5 – 3.

My head had moved through an arc of 180° as, with lip microphone pressed to my mouth, I had followed Hancock's flying figure down the touchline. I can also confirm that, contrary to the view of many a disgruntled Scot, he did not go into touch.

My first experience of an International at Twickenham was in 1931, at the age of eleven. A friend of my father took me to see England vs Wales and there was no need to get tickets in advance! We stood at the top of the old South Terrace.   All around us were Welsh miners in their red and white scarves, bitterly disappointed when B. H. Black kicked a penalty goal for England, in the closing minutes, to draw the match.

*Prince Obolensky in full flight for the try line.*

One associates a ground with its great moments. Perhaps the finest individual try at Twickenham was scored by Prince Alex Obolensky, who played for my own club, Rosslyn Park. He was on the England right wing against the New Zealand All Blacks in 1936 and got the ball ten yards inside his own half and close to the right touchline.

'Obo' was slim and very fast. He had fair hair and, in full flight, looked like a cross between a greyhound and a ghost. On this occasion he took the scenic route round the All Blacks. Having outflanked most of them, a corridor seemed to open up in front of him down which he sped to the left corner flag. England went on to win 13 – 0, with Peter Cranmer, later to be a colleague of mine in the commentary box, dropping a goal. Sadly Obo was killed in the war.

Since those days, Twickenham and the game of rugby itself have changed dramatically. High double-decker stands have arisen at both ends. In due course, both the

*Robert Hudson (left) and Peter Cranmer, former England Rugby Captain.*

East and West Stands will be rebuilt.

More important have been the changes in the laws. The game has been speeded up and made more open by sensible restriction on kicking to touch and the need to keep ten yards back at lineouts and behind the 'rear foot' at scrums.

It is a faster and better game now than when I dipped a tentative toe into the broadcasting waters at the Final Trial, England vs The Rest, at Twickenham on 20th December 1947.

I had been invited to audition as a television commentator during the second half of the game, after live transmission of the first half. In those days, when the light faded, so did the cameras. On this occasion, the light was bad from the start, and the producer, Ian Orr Ewing, took the gamble of putting me on 'live'. Accordingly, Michael Henderson handed over to me for about fifteen minutes in the first half. There is nothing like being pushed in at the deep end. All went well and I was even paid four guineas.

My first radio commentary on rugby was on the South of Scotland vs the South Africans match at Hawick in 1951. Hawick is the home town of Bill McClaren, now the leading rugby commentator, but who had not then appeared on the broadcasting scene. I wished he had, because my fellow broadcaster that day did not turn up until well into the second half. The broadcast began, ten minutes before the match started, with a preview by Jock Wemyss. Jock had played for Scotland before and after the first war, despite losing an eye during it. Then I started the commentary. By the time my missing colleague arrived, I had been talking for sixty-five minutes virtually non-stop. It was a memorable baptism, which left me hoarse and exhausted.

On joining the BBC staff in Manchester in 1954, I found myself broadcasting County Championship matches from unexpected places and came to know the meaning of "Hell, Hull and Halifax". Lancashire had a good ground at Blundellsands, where I was often joined by Harry Fry, an England international, who had played for Liverpool. At Workington, my position for Cumberland vs Lancashire was in the front row of the stand. A young lady sitting behind me turned out to be the fiancée of the Lancashire wing threequarter. He scored three tries, each greeted by a tattoo of joyous kicks in the small of my back. I suffered for Lancashire that day.

Rugby football lends itself well to radio commentary. The ebb and flow of play, with short sharp periods of fast action, interspersed by stoppages for line-outs, scrums and penalty kicks, are easier to handle, in my view, than either cricket or football. The rugby commentator can build up the suspense and interest gradually as the attacking team gains ground and approaches the opposing try-line. Tries in rugby are usually the result of sustained pressure and mounting anticipation. Andy Hancock's try, as already described, was the exception that proves the rule.

Including the referee, there are thirty-one people on a rugby field. This makes identification as difficult as it is vital. You might not recognise your own brother diving over for a try in the corner, if you had to do so from a hundred yards' range on a misty day. My lifeline was the two or three hours spent, the night before the match, learning the numbers on the players' backs. I would write these on appropriately coloured cards; for example, white for England and red for Wales. My wife, or some other unfortunate volunteer, would then hold them up at random and at high speed until I was name and number perfect. Oddly enough, they would stay in my mind while I was asleep and I could always reel them straight off in the morning. Using this method, I can say, with some pride, that I never got a try-scorer wrong in the course of broadcasting 167 rugby matches, sixty of them Internationals, on radio and television. I can recommend it with confidence!

Identification, however accurate, can be overdone. A radio commentary can sound like a telephone directory read at high speed; better by far to name the key players – "Andrew at fly-half"; then follow the ball "along the three-quarter line, going left away from us" and "out to the explosive power of Underwood on the wing".

When the scrum forms, give the reason for it, pinpoint its position, go back briefly over the last movement, signpost the options ahead, and bring in your expert summariser for a quick comment if time permits. Simple? No - but satisfying if you get it right.

The Five Nations Championship takes place at Twickenham, Murrayfield, Cardiff, Dublin and Paris. I broadcast from them all in the fifties and sixties. My routine varied from place to place. At Twickenham, I would arrive early and, no doubt illegally, go on to the field to test the going. Then an early lunch as soon as the restaurant opened and back to my car for a final check on the numbers and on my cardboard folder of notes, giving details of the players and previous matches. Then up the steep staircase of the West Stand and along the catwalk to the commentary box protruding from the front between the upper and lower decks. It is a very good position at just the right height on the halfway line. If you can't do a good commentary at Twickenham, you can't do one anywhere.

My wife often sat in the stand listening to my commentary on a transistor radio, concealed in her handbag. From this a wire emerged and led under her coat, to connect with an ear piece in her left ear. By outward appearance, she seemed deaf. At one England vs Ireland match she sat next to a slightly inebriated Irishman. When Ireland scored in the corner, everyone, except

Barbara, got up and obscured the view. "Did you see who scored that try?", asked her neighbour, without much hope of an answer. "Yes," said Barbara, " it was Kyle, from a pass by Mulcahy, about five yards from the corner flag". The Irishman reeled with astonishment (and an excess of whisky). "Amazing", he said, "you've eyes like a hawk - and you're not deaf either!"

At Murrayfield the approach to the commentary box was more hazardous: up a ladder, to a freezing position in the open. It was a splendid view if you could stop your teeth chattering.

At Cardiff, the position is more secluded nowadays, but still in the open. In my day, the crowd was all around me and it was difficult to hear my own voice in the headphones, let alone make out if it was talking sense. On several occasions, feeling very lonely as an Englishman during the singing of *Land of My Fathers*, the names and numbers of the teams seemed to melt from my brain.

Alun Williams, or G.V. Wynne Jones, would be the Welsh commentator, and it was their prerogative to take the second (and easier) twenty minutes of each half. So I had to begin. Like the teams, a commentator takes a few minutes to acclimatise, to judge pace and distance and to sort out the players. In 1963, very cold and deafened by the singing, I was more than glad to identify Malcolm Phillips, as he looped outside Peter Jackson to score England's first try, in their 13 – 6 win over Wales. That recording has had a regular airing, because England didn't win again at Cardiff for twenty-eight years!

The commentary position at Lansdowne Road, Dublin, was perhaps the best of all. Sammy Walker, former captain of the British Lions, was usually my fellow commentator. Sammy surprised me by saying that broadcasting an International match made him much more nervous than playing in one. We would walk down to the ground in a jostling good-humoured crowd, all of whom seemed to know Sammy, a true Ulsterman. The Irish rugby team is selected on merit from both North and South. If only such harmony could prevail off the field.

Stade Colombes in Paris is where Harold Abrahams won the hundred metres Gold Medal in the Olympic Games of 1924. It was also where France used to play rugby. France vs Scotland in 1957 was one of the first matches I broadcast from there. Bill McClaren and I arrived at our 'cabine' to find a marked lack of technical equipment. Eventually, two microphones and some headphones were produced, but we were still out of touch with the world. Finally, after frantic entreaties and with only seconds left before transmission, an engineer strolled up, a small cigar dangling from the side of his mouth. With an eloquent shrug of the shoulders, he connected the lines to London and left us to describe a Scottish victory.

Our commentary position was behind a portion of the stand reserved for former French internationals. When Peter Jackson scored for England in 1958, to make the score 14 – 0, loud booing and hissing broke out. I could see nothing wrong with Jackson's try. Indeed, there was not. They were booing the French selectors!

As we grow older, we tend to think the best was in the past. This may be true in cricket, but not in rugby football. The combination of wise changes in the laws, superlative fitness, competitive leagues and improved coaching

*Rugby World Cup final. England vs Australia at Twickenham, 2nd November 1991.*

methods produced, in 1991 and 1992, the best England team I can remember.

Looking back over sixty years of International rugby, one wonders who would challenge for a place in the side today. Peter Jackson would get in on the right wing, Jeff Butterfield possibly in the centre. David Duckham and Peter Cranmer would come close. H. G. Owen-Smith, who played cricket for South Africa, was a fine full back, but in those days that role was largely defensive. Richard Sharp would be a strong contender for fly-half, as would Fran Cotton, Bill Beaumont, Roger Uttley and Tony Neary among the forwards. But even they might find the pace of the game and the standard of fitness had increased since their day.

The Hastings brothers took some beating in Scotland and, for Ireland, Mike Gibson was probably the best centre threequarter anywhere. Jack Kyle too was a world-class fly-half. The great names for Wales have been Cliff Morgan, Barry John, Gareth Edwards, Gerald Davies and J. P. R. Williams. I remember the great Jean Prat of France and, more recently, the silky skills of Serge Blanco.

The fastest player I have seen on a rugby field was J. C. Gibbs of the Harlequins, and the tallest, at six feet ten inches, Peter Stagg of Scotland, although 'lamp-posts' in the lineout are more common now.

Weight, height and build dictate where you play in rugby; from bull-necked prop forwards to india-rubber scrum halves, the silhouette betrays the position. Centre threequarters tend to be about six feet tall and strongly built; the flying wingers shorter and lighter, like Rex Alston, with whom I shared the commentary box on a number of occasions, and who played for the East Midlands. The distinguished old internationals at my side, for expert opinion, have included Peter Yarranton, later President of the Rugby Union and now knighted, John Kendall-Carpenter, who died, sadly, before the 1991 World Cup, and the great Welsh full-back Vivian Jenkins. Of modern commentators, Ian Robertson, a former Scottish International, has an excellent grasp of technique and naturally sees the game with an expert eye. At one time Ian and three other Internationals, Chris Rea, Cliff Morgan and Nigel Starmer-Smith were all in my department together. We had visions of winning the Middlesex 7-a-side!

Success brings its problems and there is no doubt that Rugby Union Football is on the crest of a wave. Twickenham will arise as the finest rugby stadium in the world, and the best of any kind in Britain. The Football Association will cast envious eyes upon it. All 75,000 seats will be sold ten times over. The television audience for International matches already runs into many millions. There will be furious competition for the contract, now one of the most prized by the BBC.

Two factors intrigue me. Rugby is an intensely physical game, with a high risk of injury. The 'violence' is on the field, the spectators well behaved. The same applies to Rugby League. In football, the reverse is the case: the violence is off the field rather than on it.

The other factor is money. In Rugby Union, the players are not paid for playing, yet it is they who bring in the crowds and the cash, and who enthral millions on television and radio. I hope the ethos of amateurism can continue, but that depends on whether the stars on the field can benefit from their activities off it. Sensible ideas to this end seem to be emerging; payment for playing the game is still, rightly, barred; but the rules about lecturing, writing and advertising have been modified. So, with luck, those who have brought the game to its present popularity may share in its success. The sponsors, advertisers, hospitality experts, ticket touts, caterers, press, radio and TV all do pretty well. What about the players?

# CHAPTER 8
# Churchill: Farewell to Greatness

"We shall fight on the beaches..." had a special meaning for me, aged nineteen. I was a gunner, without any guns, so my role was to lie on the beach in my battledress, with a rifle and five rounds of ammunition. "We shall never surrender..." he said, and we knew we never would.

The cigar jutting from a cherubic face, an arm held aloft, two fingers forming the V for Victory, the Homburg hat raised on a walking stick. That was the public image. As a man, we knew him through 'The Broadcast', as he called it. He usually spoke at nine o'clock in the evening, either from 10 Downing Street or the Underground Cabinet Rooms in King Charles Street; sometimes from Chequers or Chartwell.

There was no television during the war, so the nation gathered round its wireless sets. Perhaps that other morale-raiser, Tommy Handley, with the ITMA team, would have been on the air during the previous half-hour. So we would be in good spirits. But it was Winston Churchill we wanted to hear.

Churchill did not give interviews. He made history and wrote about it afterwards, he put backbone into us all and, with his vision and leadership, we won the war. But not for him interrogation at Downing Street.

So we learn of his idiosyncrasies from others. Imagine him in bed, propped up with pillows. Papers and documents are scattered around and he is dictating to a secretary. His dog, Rufus, is lying on his feet, a ginger cat is sitting on his tummy, and a tame budgerigar on his head.

No wonder Hitler abandoned the invasion!

Churchill lived life upside-down; at his best late at night, working until two in the morning; one minute driving his staff to distraction, the next beguiling them with kindness.

Beware the humourless leader. Sir Alfred Bossom was a new Member of Parliament. "What an extraordinary name," said Churchill, "neither one thing nor the other."

He was the holder of virtually every high office in the land. As a young man, he had charged at Omdurman; as an old one, he had saved the Free World. When he died, the nation prepared to honour him with a massive display of gratitude.

The chimes of Big Ben at half-past nine died away down Whitehall and the voice of John Snagge began our broadcast with words so familiar in wartime, "This is London". It was 30th January 1965 and the start of the only State Funeral of a 'commoner' this century.

*State Funeral of Sir Winston Churchill. The Cortege in Whitehall, en route to St Paul's.*

Some commoner!

For many months we in the BBC had consulted the file containing details of the funeral arrangements. It was labelled Hope-Not. Lines had been laid, cameras and microphone positions organised, commentators and engineers warned to be ready. The State Funeral of Sir Winston Churchill was about to begin.

It was my forty-fifth birthday and I was to give the radio commentary from St Paul's. The day was cold and dry and, as I drove from Broadcasting House early in the morning, people were already standing ten to twelve deep on the pavements. I reflected that I was exactly half the age of the man to whom we owed so much. The BBC radio team had all served in the war. Raymond Baxter, now in Trafalgar square, had been a fighter pilot and Audrey Russell, outside St Paul's, Godfrey Talbot at Tower Pier, and Wynford Vaughan Thomas, up river at Festival Hall, had been distinguished war correspondents. I had been seven years in the army.

Churchill's body had lain in State in Westminster Hall as the people of London filed past in their thousands. Now the Bearer Party of Guardsmen lifted the heavy coffin onto a gun carriage and a ninety-gun salute – one for each year of Churchill's life – boomed out from St James's Park. On the coffin lay the insignia of a Knight of the Garter.

The funeral procession was threequarters of a mile long; 122 officers and 2,299 other ranks took part in it. I remember, as if it was yesterday, the sound of the slow tramp of feet coming through my headphones as I sat in the West Gallery of St Paul's. A listener in Pakistan wrote later:

> We felt we were in London, joining the rest of the world
> in a humble tribute to Greatness. We felt the cold
> stillness and the strange magic that London holds. The
> Service, the Bugles, the Pipers all came to us with
> remarkable clarity.

In pride of place walked the Battle of Britain aircrews. Then came the Royal Horse Artillery, the five Guards Regiments, the Royal Marines and the Royal Navy. It took an hour for the procession to reach St Paul's. The gun carriage was pulled by

*The State Funeral of Sir Winston Churchill in St Paul's Cathedral, 30th January 1965.*

140 sailors. The Earl Marshal, the Duke of Norfolk, walked in front of it. At intervals down the long column, eight bands played. "We heard every sound, every breath and movement," wrote an expatriate from Spain.

Certain pictures, from inside St Paul's, remain sharply in my mind: the coffin, draped in the Union Jack and with three tall, orange candles on either side, lying directly beneath the dome; the Queen, pale-faced and in a black coat and hat, standing with Prince Philip; a youthful Prince Charles, who had come from school at Gordonstoun for the funeral service; the tall, gaunt figure of General de Gaulle staring fixedly ahead; the strain on the faces of the young Guardsmen carrying the heavy lead-lined coffin. Nearly 150 countries were represented. I was given plenty of time to set the majestic scene and give details of the congregation and the service as the procession wound its slow way down Whitehall, through Trafalgar Square to Fleet Street and up Ludgate Hill.

There were three stirring hymns, chosen, so we understood, by Churchill himself. *He who would valiant be*, was later followed by *The Battle Hymn of the Republic* ('Mine eyes have seen the glory of the coming of the Lord'), which contains the lines, 'He hath sounded forth the trumpet that shall never call retreat' and, in the last verse, 'As he died to make men holy, let us die to make men

free'. The scene was one of rich solemnity and the hymns were sung with pride and love.

Finally, after the National Anthem, *Last Post* and *Reveillé*, came the procession down the Nave, led by the Heralds and Pursuivants in their tabards of scarlet and gold, muted by a black sash, with Churchill's honours and decorations carried on velvet cushions. As the procession came slowly towards me in the West Gallery, his favourite hymn *O God, our help in ages past* was sung and I quoted the lines, 'Time, like an ever-rolling stream, bears all its sons away', as the West Doors were opened and the shafts of morning light filtered in to enfold the coffin. In front of it walked the distinguished Pall Bearers, whose names read today like a roll call of modern history: Mountbatten, Alexander, Eden, Menzies, Ismay, Macmillan, Portal, Attlee, Bridges, Slim, Normanbrook and Templer.

For me, it was a moment of great emotion and yet, somehow, I had to try to give expression to the thoughts of those listening in Britain and around the world. For younger generations, it must be hard to appreciate how we, who had been through the Blitz and the war, felt at that time. First was pride "to have lived with him in the hour of danger," then gratitude "for all he had done for us and for freedom," and finally sadness that we "shall never see him, or his like, again".

As the cortège went slowly on through the City to Tower Pier, Sir Robert Menzies, Prime Minister of Australia, spoke on behalf of the Commonwealth, with the muffled bells of St Paul's ringing in the background:

"When we stood at the gates of destiny in 1940 and 1941, one man won a victory for human freedom. We thank him and we thank God for him. In future years we will be proud to say, 'I lived in Churchill's time'."

My part in the broadcast was now over, but Richard Dimbleby, in the television commentary box next to me, still had much to do. The coffin was laid gently on the Port of London Authority launch *Havengore* and, escorted by river police, the little flotilla crept "slowly away up the last of the tide". Royal Air Force Lightnings roared over the river in salute and, in an unforgettable gesture, the arms of the huge mechanical cranes along the shore dipped in unison.

It was at Blenheim Palace that Winston Churchill took two major decisions: in his own words, "to be born and to marry". Now his third decision, to be buried near his family in the little church at Bladon within sight of Blenheim, was to take effect.

The coffin was taken by train from Waterloo to Long Handborough station near Bladon, then to the unpretentious little church and to the grave next to his mother, who had been to him "like the Evening Star". We, in radio, had considered having a commentator in the house at the entrance to the churchyard but, in the end, rejected it as being too intrusive.

There was, however, a television camera and Richard Dimbleby continued to speak from St Paul's. He finished by reading a poem by Avril Anderson:

From the Hall of Kings they bore him then
The greatest of all Englishmen
To the nation's, the world's requiem
At Bladon.

So Churchill sleeps; yet surely wakes
Old Warrior, where the morning breaks
On sunlit uplands – but the heart aches,
At Bladon.

# CHAPTER 9
# Welsh Interlude

"I intend to create my son, Charles, Prince of Wales today. When he is grown up, I will present him to you at Caernarvon."

This was Her Majesty the Queen speaking at the Closing Ceremony of the Empire Games in Cardiff in 1958, but not in person; on tape. She was unwell. The recording had been made at Windsor and conveyed in great secrecy by a BBC courier to a rendezvous near Gloucester where it was handed to a representative of BBC Wales, who brought the precious parcel to Cardiff. Even Alun Williams, who described the closing ceremony on the radio, did not know the content of the tape. However, the engineer transmitting it was briefed, at the last moment, to stop the machine after the word 'today', to allow a great roar from the crowd, before re-starting it, so that the Queen's final sentence could be heard clearly. It seems that the nine-year-old Prince Charles, listening with school friends in his Headmaster's study at Cheam, was as surprised as everyone else.

This would be the first time that an Investiture of a Prince of Wales had been broadcast: the last one was in 1911 and took place, out of public view, in a green and white tent inside the Castle.

The BBC had two years' warning. The date, set in 1967, was to be 1st July, 1969. It would be a television spectacular in colour. Lord Snowdon, appointed in 1964 as Constable of Caernarvon Castle, set about cleaning it up with good effect. An expert photographer, and nephew of Oliver Messel the theatre designer, he forged an effective alliance with Antony Craxton, one of the BBC's most perceptive producers.

Radio was less enthusiastic. It would be a 'non-event' – and partly in Welsh, to make matters worse. It might mean cancelling *Woman's Hour*. Its probable two-hour duration did nothing to sugar the pill. Finally, the 'live' broadcast was placed on the Third Network (Radio 3), with an edited version later in the evening on the Home Service (Radio 4).

In the event, nearly two million listened to the radio in this country, and many more overseas. The worldwide television audience was, of course, colossal. The Appreciation Index for both radio and television was extremely high.

I had been Head of Outside Broadcasts for only six months, so this unique occasion was my first big challenge. I wasted no time in visiting Caernarvon and assessing the problems involved in fitting modern technology, commentators and engineers into an ancient castle. The activities of the Welsh Nationalists were also causing acute security problems. A meeting was held in London to co-ordinate the broadcasting and press arrangements.

"Will Her Majesty know that the microphones are being carried out to the dais by a Sergeant in the Welsh Guards?" My tentative question was addressed to the formidable figure of the Earl Marshal, the Duke of Norfolk. "The Queen," he replied, and I was glad to note a twinkle in his eyes, "will know everything". And so it was and always is. As this was to be a State Occasion, the Duke, as Earl Marshal, was in charge of the organisation as a whole. His problems must have included not only protocol but security, timing and, not least I imagine, briefing the Queen, Prince Philip and Prince Charles about a ceremony which none of them had ever seen and which, in any case, had not taken place for fifty-eight years.

The procedure on the slate dais, with its four steps up from the grass and with a perspex roof manoeuvred through the castle gate with two inches to spare, was rehearsed on the flat lawns of Buckingham Palace, with bits of string as guidelines. Orchestras, choirs, bands and trumpeters all went through their paces separately, as did the processions inside and outside the castle. For my part, I made sure that Sergeant Reeves practised carrying the microphones to a spot marked with a small piece of tape on the dais. This was just as well because, at rehearsal, he did this with such military enthusiasm that the cable came out of its socket.

Meanwhile, I had arranged for a true Welshman, Alun Williams, to give the main commentary (in English) from the lofty heights of the Chamberlain Tower. On the day he was accompanied by two plain-clothes police officers, who had chosen it as a security vantage point. Other broadcasters, speaking in Welsh, were stationed on the battlements below. Fifteen commentators, from the BBC's own Language Services and from foreign broadcasting organisations, were strung along the ramparts; each had a TV monitor screen to circumvent the awkward shape of the castle and to see the processions outside it. Our engineers, rather to their dismay, were consigned to what appeared to be a dungeon.

Visual control for the 'mixing' of sound and speech was essential and we were lucky to find a window in the Black Tower, which overlooked the dais. From here Don Eustace, one of our senior Outside Broadcast engineers 'fed' a carefully-balanced mixture of music, singing and fanfares, and of speech in English and Welsh, not only to radio, but also to television and to all overseas organisations. Each service added its own commentaries separately.

Lt. Col. Jaeger, Senior Director of Music of the Household Division, and an old friend of mine, had his problems as well, with bands and trumpeters dotted round the walls. It was decided to station a second conductor on the roof of the

Post Office in the main square. This allowed the trumpeters to face outwards when the Queen presented the new Prince of Wales to the crowds outside at Queen Eleanor's Gate.

The engineers excelled themselves in running cables and installing microphones in all parts of the castle, so that the fanfares of trumpeters, perched precariously on turrets and battlements, would be heard worldwide. It was a technical tour de force.

We took over a school for the News output and Godfrey Talbot gave a succession of reports throughout the day from what was, in fact, a broom cupboard. The BBC party occupied the University hostel at Bangor, a few miles away, where I finalised the detailed running order with Arthur Phillips, my deputy. On the morning of the Investiture itself I took an early train back to London. My place was in the Continuity Suite in Broadcasting House in case some disaster occurred at Caernarvon and carefully prepared programme changes would have to be put into effect.

I left behind me a scene of elegant simplicity. The Duke of Norfolk was a fine organiser, but an astute delegator as well. He had given Lord Snowdon virtually a free hand within the castle. The grey walls were set off to perfection by the central carpet of grass, encouraged, by skilful means, to grow to a luxuriant green and with not even a red carpet permitted to mar its pristine state. Against this background the red Dragons of Wales, on white banners, hung from the walls. The Gentlemen at Arms in their scarlet uniforms, with white swans' feathers protruding from silver helmets, would stand guard round the contrasting modernity of the grey slate dais. Here stood three chairs, also of Welsh slate. Only the Queen's had a back to it; a clue to the absolute priority of design for television.

Nothing was allowed to spoil the perfect picture. The musical conductors would not stand on podia but at ground level; an awning over the grass, as protection against the rain, was ruled out. There would be no canopy at Water Gate, where the Queen would enter the castle.

The BBC made three different microphone designs and, by placing Lord Snowdon's preferred choice a little in front of the other two, persuaded the Duke of Norfolk to choose it. The four thousand people inside the castle sat on vermilion-coloured chairs, complementing perfectly the grey walls and green grass. If it rained, they would get wet. The chairs were all sold afterwards for £12 each!

Television cameras were fixed, not on the battlements, but on hoists. They rose to take their pictures and then disappeared again behind the castle walls. In that way the media remained unobtrusive, yet the picture perfect to you in your armchair. Circumstances were not quite so good though for some in the Lower Ward of the castle, whose view of the proceedings was obstructed by the Chamberlain Tower. Lord Snowdon solved this problem by providing convex plastic looking-glasses. Possibly his only mistake was to wear a dark green tailcoat, which resembled a pantomime 'Buttons'. But it was a minor blemish – like the rain, which kept away until near the end. Only one person put on a raincoat.

I took my place in the Continuity Suite at Broadcasting House with some trepidation, not about the broadcast, which had been planned thoroughly and was in good hands, but about the security arrangements. My morale was not improved by a loud bang at the start of the programme. This turned out to be the first salvo of a 21-gun salute, on the arrival of the Royal Train at Griffiths Crossing, two miles from Caernarvon.

Soon, Raymond Baxter, in Caernarvon Square, was describing the first of the Royal Processions and I began to breathe more easily. The journey from Griffiths Crossing, in open carriages, was regarded as the most obvious target for Welsh Nationalist activity. Emergency action had been carefully laid down, but I had no wish to put it into effect.


The broadcast is going well. Here comes Prince Charles with his Escort of Forty Household Cavalry and we hear *God Bless the Prince of Wales*, splendidly sung, as he makes his way to a specially-prepared room in the Chamberlain Tower, to await the arrival of his mother.

Next, a full Sovereign's Escort comes clattering up to Water Gate and the Queen and Prince Philip look on with some amusement as Lord Plunkett, an Equerry, ascends the sixteen steps and hammers on the castle door – "I demand admission in the name of the Queen," he shouts. To pick this up we use what is known as a 'gun mike' fixed above the door. I have explained to the horrified police that it is not really a gun.

Now Lord Snowdon comes out with a large fake key, about fifteen inches long, on a cushion, which tends to add to the pantomime effect of his costume. He surrenders the key to the Queen, who sensibly returns it.

The Royal Procession makes its way to the dais, the Queen in yellow, Prince Philip in military uniform. Prince Charles is summoned by Garter King of Arms from the Chamberlain Tower. He wears the uniform of Colonel-in-Chief of the Royal Regiment of Wales. *Land of my Fathers* is sung as only the Welsh can, followed by *God Save the Queen*. Soon Prince Charles is invested with a rather spiky-looking crown, a ring, a golden rod and a mantle.

Mr James Callaghan reads the Letters Patent and the Prince replies to the loyal address in (apparently) excellent Welsh, as well as in English. There follows a religious service in both languages.

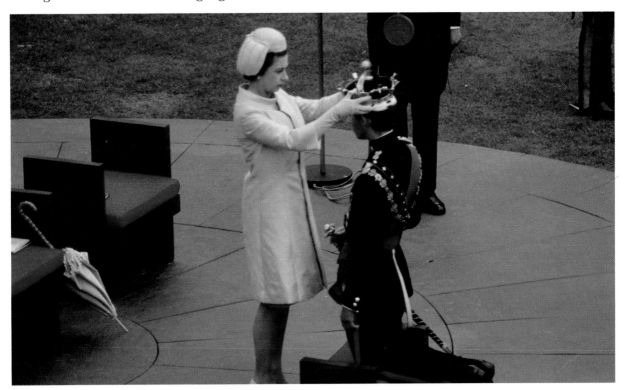

*The Investiture of the Prince of Wales, Prince Charles, at Caernarvon Castle on 1st July 1969.*

The Queen makes three 'presentations', holding the hand of the newly-invested Prince of Wales. First to those outside at Queen Eleanor's Gate, then at Kings Gate and, finally, for those in the castle, in the Lower Ward. Each time, the fanfares dovetail perfectly with the commentaries. Our timing is good; the engineers, as always, technically excellent.

Raymond Baxter describes the Royal Procession leaving Caernarvon Square. We fade the programme and a remarkable chapter of history is over.

An ancient castle has lent itself to an historic ceremony, performed largely for a huge audience watching and listening in absentia all over the world. It has been a triumphant success and, thank goodness, no disaster has occurred.

I heave a sigh of relief. A cup of tea, in the BBC canteen, tastes like champagne.

# CHAPTER 10
# Today

"After the nine o'clock news, there will be a talk by Sir John Macpherson on 'The Land of the Nigger'."

Jack de Manio, the BBC continuity announcer in Broadcasting House, felt a moment of unease. He pressed the key connecting him to the control cubicle. "Shouldn't that have been 'Niger'?" he asked, a hint of panic in his voice. "I rather think it should," replied the studio manager.

It was 29th January 1956. Jack de Manio, in his book *To Auntie with Love*, does not pretend that it was this gaffe-of-the-century alone which propelled him to fame and a place in Madame Tussaud's waxworks exhibition, but it certainly helped.

At Government House, Lagos, the scene was one of frozen incredulity. The Governor, who had recorded his talk, and Nigeria's leading political figures, were gathered in the drawing room to listen to it. Independence for Nigeria was still four years away. Wynford Vaughan Thomas was the BBC representative. Every face in the room, black and white, turned in his direction. "He will be sacked of course?" said a particularly grave face. "At once," said Wynford desperately, "in fact, he probably has been already".

Wynford was overestimating the BBC's speed of decision in these matters. It was very difficult to get the sack. Jack was sent home, while the BBC considered what to do with him. He was moved first to the Overseas Service; an odd decision, as he would now be speaking much more frequently to the country he had just insulted. Finally, as so often happens, he was shunted sideways to some unimportant little magazine programme which had been started in the early morning on the Home Service. That programme was *Today*.

*Robin Day*

The idea had come to a newly-joined Talks Producer called (appropriately) Day – now Sir Robin. On arrival he had been informed that in Features, they wore sports jackets; in Drama, painful though this was to contemplate, they wore corduroy trousers; "but in Talks we wear suits".

Suitably attired, he noticed that nothing much seemed to happen on the radio in the mornings. Six and a half million people were listening to the 8.00 am News on the Home Service, but then had to subsist on a diet of light music, *Lift Up Your Hearts* and the weather forecast until another bulletin at 9 o'clock. The Light Programme didn't start until then anyway.

In his book *Grand Inquisitor*, Sir Robin Day includes the memorandum sent to his boss on 7th July 1955. This suggested a format for the programme, which has taken the nation by the ears for thirty-five years and has seen off the challenge of early morning television.

A few months later, as I have recounted in Chapter 4, I was to write a memorandum to my own boss, suggesting ball-by-ball coverage of Test Matches on the Third Network. *Today* and *Test Match Special*, two radio programmes which have become, in their own way, national institutions, eventually took to the air in 1957.

Jack de Manio was a gregarious and amusing character who saw no reason to go to bed early just because five million people would be hanging on to his every word in the morning. In those days, *Today* was really a light-hearted magazine programme which 'reflected' the news of the day, when it felt like it, but usually concerned itself with eccentrics who ate light bulbs or pedalled across the channel. There were two editions. The first was from 7.15 to 7.45, after the 7.00 am News and a review of the papers. The second was from 8.15 to 8.40. Breakfast was served between the two, while the producer considered what alterations could usefully be made. Among all this harmless fun, the 'time-check' assumed critical importance. The Nation would otherwise miss its train and might fail to see the joke.

The snag was that Jack often got the time wrong.

Various reasons for this have been advanced. Some even suggested that he

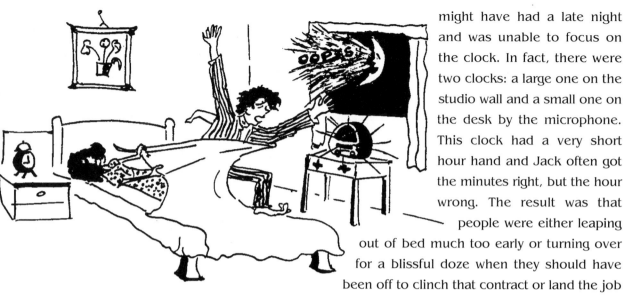

might have had a late night and was unable to focus on the clock. In fact, there were two clocks: a large one on the studio wall and a small one on the desk by the microphone. This clock had a very short hour hand and Jack often got the minutes right, but the hour wrong. The result was that people were either leaping out of bed much too early or turning over for a blissful doze when they should have been off to clinch that contract or land the job of their dreams – which might now prove to be just that.

In those days, there was only one presenter and the arrangement was that Jack would do two months on and one month off. The third month was covered by either Brian Johnston, John Timpson, Martin Muncaster or myself. We all made quite a good job of it, but none of us, it would be fair to say, possessed the eccentric and fallible charm of Jack de Manio. The more Jack rustled his papers, fluffed his lines and told people the wrong time, the more warmly entrenched he became in the hearts of his audience.

In the sixties, when I joined the programme, our chief bugbear was the 'opt out'. This involved some English and National regions leaving and rejoining the programme at various predetermined and exact times.

I recall a live interview leading up to the 8.30 opt out. My interviewee, not forthcoming at first, was getting handsomely into his stride, encouraged, no doubt, by my warm smile of approval. Only one thing is more difficult than getting people to talk on the air, and that is persuading them to stop. The look of injured innocence on the face of this particular person haunts me still as, with one eye on the clock, I interrupted his happy flow – "And finally, Mr So-and-So, and *very* briefly...". A useful tip for interviewers is never to ask a question to which the answer is "Yes" or "No" – unless of course you are confronted by an opt out!

Listeners were naturally unable to fathom the reason for these abrupt endings, made for the benefit of engineers in Birmingham, Bristol or Cardiff, so that lines could be switched and the regional programme begin on time. A recorded item, preceding an opt out, had to have alternative 'out cues', and the producer, however accurate his mental arithmetic, would often leave the presenter with an awkward twenty seconds. Thus was born the 'filler' industry.

The first thing I did in the morning was to collect, from the newsroom along the corridor, a trayful of potential fillers: odd happenings from all over the world which had come in from the News Agencies during the night. These I would sub-edit down to ten-, twenty- or thirty-second lengths, so as to be ready for any emergency. John Timpson later solved the problem very neatly by inviting listeners to send in what he called 'Ho-Hos', which they did in their thousands. Most were extracts from local papers; 'Crash Course for Learner Drivers' was a nice example.

Sudden deaths and telephone interviews were two additional hazards. A singing star was reported dead too late for the News, but in time for *Today*. With commendable speed our solitary secretary collected a recording of one of the star's songs from the Record Library. With seconds to spare, we opened the programme with it. It was *Pennies from Heaven*.

I like interviewing, if I can see who I am talking to; this is not the case on the telephone. Life becomes very difficult if, in addition, you have no knowledge of the subject under discussion. A case in point was a coastguard in Cornwall who apparently thought I knew all about the wreck of a yacht on his stretch of the coast. I didn't, but was hoping he would tell me. This he did, after much prompting, and with an 'opt out' looming ominously.

Listeners are astonishingly quick to correct mistakes. They reach for the telephone, their mouths still full of cornflakes. One morning, my script had placed a small north-eastern village in Northumberland: we were at once bombarded with calls telling us it was in Durham. It was nice to know they were awake – and listening.

The five-minute review of the day's papers was compiled in the Newsroom and read by an announcer from the *Today* studio at 8.40 am, when our second edition finished. One morning, with thirty seconds to go before the end of the programme, no announcer having appeared, the producer, Bob Craddock, rushed into the studio with what appeared to be the bottom 'flimsy' copy of the *Today's Papers* script. "Read that," he said, and beat a hasty retreat.

The script, held in reserve for such an emergency, had obviously only been on casual terms with the carbon paper and was extremely difficult to decipher. Nor did I know what unpronounceable names might be lurking within it. All I did know was that I had a maximum of five minutes to read it. It was a minor triumph of my broadcasting career – I completed the course in four minutes fifty-nine seconds without making a mistake, despite the fact that, for the final two minutes, the agonised face of the announcer was peering at me through a window in the studio door. He had overslept.

On the evening before my first appearance on *Today*, I recorded an interview with Anita Harris, who was then a rising singing star; on another occasion, it was a great pleasure to talk to Andy Sandham, the great Surrey and England batsman who had opened the innings so often with Jack Hobbs, to whom he referred as 'The Master'. Ted Dexter and Clement Freud also figured among more than sixty people to whom I had the opportunity of speaking on the programme.

Steve Bonarjee was the mastermind of the first twelve years of *Today*, and of much more besides, including the coverage of General Elections. The script for *Today* was written by the producer, who also assembled and edited the programme during the night. He had a tough job. The presenter did not have to be in the studio until 6.30. I had a short stroll across the road from my hotel in Hallam Street.

But changes were afoot. I became Head of Outside Broadcasts in 1969, and my congenial association with the programme was at an end. The plans for broadcasting in the seventies were to bring an altogether sharper look to *Today*. It was now to reflect all sections of a newspaper, not just the feature pages.

John Timpson, a newsman, was brought in on a permanent basis to partner Jack de Manio and give the programme 'backbone'. So began an amiable, but doomed, fusion of the old and new eras. *Today* would never be the same again.

Many people have to get up early in the morning: one thinks of milkmen, postmen, refuse collectors and train drivers. However, such people do not have to untangle the overnight news, nor put searching questions to a cabinet minister about a treaty signed in Brussels in the middle of the night.

The amalgamation of News and Current Affairs and the continuous nature of the programme, now extended to two and a half hours, has meant that two presenters – and high calibre ones at that – are essential.

The programme would now include not only recorded 'packages' from reporters around the world but, increasingly, contributions from studios round the country, outside broadcast points and mobile radio cars. The telephone would track down a key contributor wherever he might be in the world, and live appearances in the studio would increase.

Aspects of the news would be analysed and discussed with those who form opinions and make decisions. Cabinet ministers rarely refuse to take part. Mrs Thatcher was apparently a regular listener, so the programme then served as a direct line to 'the boss'. Sports and financial news have become regular features and *Thought for the Day* has a topical flavour. Weather and traffic information blends in with the news bulletins and summaries.

John Timpson and Robert Robinson were the first to master the new format; then Brian Redhead joined Timpson in 1975. Finally, Redhead, John Humphrys and Sue Macgregor became the leading trio of an alternating rota in the nineties.

They are in the studio by 4.45 am, write their own scripts and decide how to tackle the interviews they will be doing in the next two and a half hours.

On 26th May 1992, some thirty years after my own first appearance, I visited the *Today* studio, during the transmission of the programme.

*Today* is broadcast from a studio on the fourth floor of Broadcasting House. I arrive at 7.15 am, when it has been on the air for forty-five minutes, and so is well into its stride. The presenters are Brian Redhead and John Humphrys.

On the other side of the glass panel, a staff of five produce the programme.

A senior Editor is in ultimate control of the content. The Producer and the Studio Manager look after the minute-by-minute details, lining up recorded contributions, incoming telephone calls and outside broadcast points. Material on tape is deftly handled by a young man and a young woman, working under pressure with a sure touch. They tell the producer, to the second, when each tape will end. Young women seem particularly good at this job, which demands manual dexterity and a quick brain.

Visitors to the studio are ushered in, about five minutes before they are due on the air, by the Production Assistant on duty. The news bulletins are read from the *Today* studio, unlike in my day, when they were quite separate. The newsreader is Charlotte Green, who also reads the review of the morning papers.

During the ten-minute bulletin, Brian Redhead comes out of the studio to tell me that he hopes to complete twenty years on *Today* in 1995, when he will be sixty-five. He is a great asset to the programme. It must be daunting to be confronted by such a lively and penetrating intellect so early in the morning! But he is very kind to the less experienced. John Humphrys, too, has a polite way of getting to the point, and I have long thought Sue Macgregor the best interviewer in the business.

Technology has improved and increased since my time. The studio console looks like the flight deck of an airliner. Monitor screens display mysterious information. It is all smoothly efficient.

Anyone unused to a broadcasting studio would be surprised at the constant flow of information from the producer and editor into the presenters' headphones. Visiting broadcasters do not wear these, unless they need to hear what a distant contributor is saying in order to join in a discussion. The chatter will be about the *next* item: the present one, on tape, is virtually ignored unless it goes on too long. The clock is the master.

There is a general air of calm professionalism. Nobody gets very excited. Indeed, the only problem is a shaky line from Lisbon. Brian Redhead perks up when Garry Richardson comes in with the sports news, and a bit of banter is possible, not least about the racing tips which haven't won. Otherwise, the troubles in Northern Ireland, the fighting in Yugoslavia and the economic situation don't offer much scope for levity. The trouble with news is that it is mostly bad.

Listen to *Today* for an hour and you will be as up to date as it is possible to be. You will know what's in the papers and, with luck, what will win the 3.30 at Ascot. You will be told which roads to avoid and which trains are not running. *Thought for the Day* will have given you something to think about and you will have been warned about the weather. You will have heard people with authority and knowledge speaking on the topics of the day.

All this doesn't happen by accident, nor just between 6.30 and 9.00 am. The really hard work is done in the twenty-four hours before 6.30. The editorial decisions on what to cover, how and with whom to do it, together with the organisation of worldwide technical and human resources, make up a formidable challenge. We hear the well-known presenters, but most of the work is done behind the scenes. The programme is a far cry from the days of Jack de Manio, in the fifties and sixties, but it is brilliantly created and presented, and has won award after award. It will continue to do so.

In my day, as I have suggested, we sent people off to work much less well-informed and, quite possibly, at the wrong time. Yet they tended to have the ghost of a smile on their faces.

In a somewhat sombre world, that can be a useful asset.

# CHAPTER 11
# Remembrance Sunday

The Cenotaph Service in Whitehall, on Remembrance Sunday, presents the radio commentator with a unique challenge. All the normal rules of commentary of course apply: to relate the description to your own position, to create a picture in the mind and to describe the event as it unfolds within that framework. The significant parts of the music and the whole of the religious service must be heard without interruption. All this is normal practice.

But at the Cenotaph, there is an added unseen dimension. On this day, untold thousands – many living alone – are thinking of a husband, a father or grandfather, a brother or a friend who died in one of the two World Wars or in one of the more recent conflicts. A fading photograph on the mantelpiece will revive memories of the past. The broadcast should bring reassurance, as far as it can, that the death was not in vain and, above all, that those who did not come back will never be forgotten.

So the radio commentator has, in a sense, a pastoral role to play; his words, dropping precisely into place, must strike exactly the right note. The mental image of the scene and the personal recollections prompted by his words can often be more vivid and satisfying than any television picture, however skillfully composed.

I know, from first-hand experience, that radio can be the bearer of a comforting message, as the many letters I received from all over the world, between 1962 and 1984, have testified. My correspondents have included the daughter of one of the founder members of the Royal British Legion, and a former Brigade Major, still treasuring the 'pink signal' received at his headquarters, at 9.38 am on 11th November 1918, announcing that hostilities would cease at eleven o'clock. No signal can have been more welcome.

My own personal memory is of a study at school, in the late thirties, shared with three other boys. I was the oldest, and so in charge. None of the other

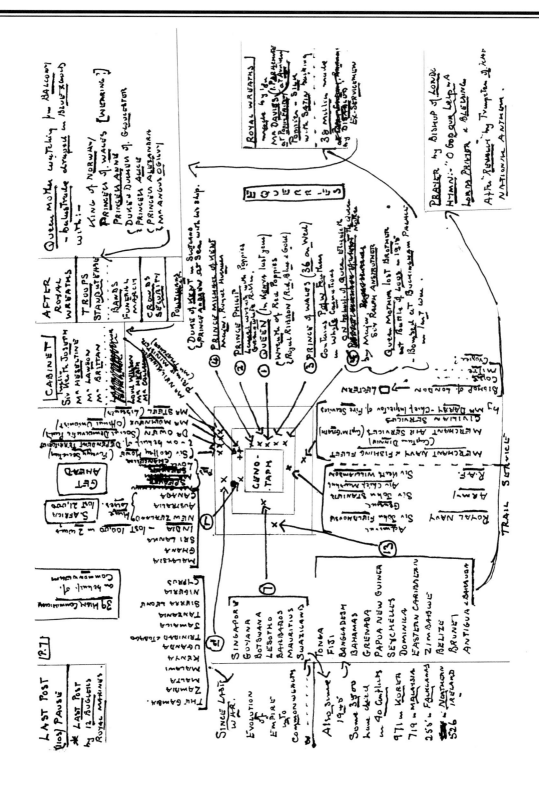

three reached his twenty-first birthday: one, a Pilot Officer, was shot down in the Battle of Britain; another, who became Head of the School, was drowned in the Atlantic when his ship was torpedoed; the third, who played in the football eleven, was killed while storming ashore in Sicily with the commandos.

Before the broadcast at the Cenotaph I liked to sit quietly in my commentary position and say a little prayer for those young men and for all my colleagues in the Army who were killed in the last war. I prayed too that the broadcast I was about to give would, in a small way, help the cause of peace and bring some comfort to those who needed it.

Then emotion had to be brought under control to tackle the professional task ahead and submit to the discipline of the stop-watch.

It was not easy.

I remember when I was a boy in the twenties and everything – and everybody – stopped for the two minutes' silence. I often thought how terrible the First World War must have been, a view confirmed by my father's ill-health, the latent legacy of gas and shell shock.

In the Second War, I, like my father, served in the Royal Horse Artillery, and also experienced the London Blitz. This background has helped me to put Remembrance Sunday in perspective. I have often felt that a younger man, however competent, would find the broadcast much more difficult.

My preparations followed similar lines each year. I would visit the Royal British Legion and also their Poppy Factory at Richmond in Surrey. There I would examine the beautiful Royal Wreaths, the poppies made of silk on a satin background, talk to their makers and check the total number of poppies produced during the year by the disabled ex-Service men and women who work there. In 1984, when I last took part in the broadcast, the figure was thirty-eight million, an echo of the carnage in the poppy fields of Flanders in the first World War.

A Canadian doctor, Colonel John McCrae, wrote these words in the dug-out, which served as his field dressing station, during the second battle of

Ypres. They found their way into *Punch* magazine:

In Flanders fields the poppies blow,
Between the crosses, row on row
That mark our place; and in the sky
The larks still bravely singing fly
Scarce heard amid the guns below.

We are the dead. Short days ago
We lived, felt dawn, saw sunset glow,
Loved and were loved, and now we lie
        In Flanders fields.

Take up our quarrel with the foe;
To you from failing hands we throw
The torch; be yours to hold it high,
If ye break faith with us who die
We shall not sleep, though poppies grow
        In Flanders fields.

An American lady, Moina Michael, was moved to make the following reply:

Oh! You who sleep in Flanders fields
Sleep sweet – to rise anew;
We caught the torch you threw,
And holding high we kept
The faith with those who died.

And now the torch and poppy red
Wear in honour of our dead.
Fear not that ye have died for naught;
We've learned the lesson that ye taught
        In Flanders fields.

Thus the poppy became the emblem of Remembrance.

At the Legion's Head Office, I would get details of the march past of Legion members, which follows the service at the Cenotaph and which seems to get bigger rather than smaller each year. The Poppy Appeal is of crucial importance to nearly half a million people who are disabled. I always devoted part of my commentary, at a suitable point, to the work of the Legion.

On many occasions it fell to me to broadcast the Festival of Remembrance at the Albert Hall on the evening prior to the Cenotaph Service. On those occasions I would stay the night in London. Otherwise, it would mean an early train from my home in St Albans on the Sunday morning, then a taxi to the Field of Remembrance in the precincts of Westminster Abbey. Here, since 1928, crosses have been planted in memory of each unit of the Army and on behalf of the Royal Navy and Royal Air Force. I would pause by the plot of grass dedicated to the Royal Artillery and then walk on up Whitehall to the Cenotaph.

Soon, I would be back in the real world where the crowds would already be twelve deep on the pavements on either side of the road, and my briefcase would be searched by an affable but punctilious policeman: security seemed to increase year by year, and rightly so.

Our Outside Broadcasts van is parked in a mews on the east side of Whitehall; inside it, I go through the details of the broadcast with the engineers and the producer, John Haslam or Caroline Elliot. We agree the points at which cue-light signals will be given so that the sound effects may be reduced behind my voice. We also confirm the action to be taken in case of a disturbance during the Two Minutes' Silence. The agreed policy in radio, in my time, was to ignore any minor demonstration, but to refer to it after the Silence. Only in the event of a direct attack on a member of the Royal Family would the commentator break into the Silence and describe what was happening. Television viewers of course would be seeing it anyway.

For many years my commentary position was a window in a Government Office building overlooking the Cenotaph. Later, when they started to knock it down, the BBC moved outside on the scaffolding. I reflected that Charles the

First had lost his head in a similar position further up Whitehall.

At ten o'clock, timing being vital, I start two stop-watches – in case one breaks down. At 10.15 I note that they are both still exactly in agreement with Big Ben. Meanwhile, the troops, with their Bands, are marching up Whitehall to form that familiar pattern round the white Portland stone of the Cenotaph, which stands like a solitary sentry in the middle of the road. On it are three words: 'The Glorious Dead'.

We are due on the air at half past ten. By then, the Royal Navy and the Royal Marines, in white helmets and khaki greatcoats, should be lining the far side of the road. The Queen's Colour Squadron of the Royal Air Force will be marching up Whitehall to join them. The road itself will be completely filled by six of the finest military bands in the world. In 1984, they were the Bands of the Scots, Welsh, Irish and Coldstream Guards, comprising a mass of grey greatcoats, black bearskin caps and softly gleaming instruments. The music is at first stirring, then evocative, wistful and sad. In front stand the four Drum Majors, in frock coats of gold lace and black velvet caps. To support them, in the rear, are the Bands of the Royal Marines and the Royal Air Force.

On the near side to me, dismounted troopers of the Life Guards, with white plumes in silver helmets, vie with the eye-catching black and gold busbys of the 'Kings Troop' Royal Horse Artillery, so named personally by King George VI on a visit to their barracks at St John's Wood. Next come the Coldstream Guards and then the red berets of the Territorial Battalion of the Parachute Regiment, together with the Women's Services and the nurses. Finally, a large combined detachment of the civilian services, including the police, ambulancemen, firemen and Red Cross workers, come marching up to complete three sides of the square. I look over their heads. It is 10.30.

"This is Radio Four and the World Service of the BBC..." The voice of the announcer comes into my headphones and I raise the 'lip microphone', as it is called, to my mouth. Now it is up to me. Nobody will paint a picture, unless I do.

I have six minutes until, at 10.36 exactly, Lieutenant Colonel Dick Ridings will mount the rostrum, in the middle of the road, to conduct the bands. He is an old friend. We have agreed that he will keep his baton raised for several seconds to give me the clearest possible signal that *Rule Britannia* is about to reverberate down Whitehall. For a moment I think his arms have got stuck – but the timing is perfect. I stop; the bands start.

The mood is triumphant: *Hearts of Oak*, *Men of Harlech*; after all, we won. Then the price we paid is reflected by the music: *Flowers of the Forest* by the Pipers, Elgar's incomparable *Nimrod* and, finally, *Solemn Melody*. I say little during the music except to identify it. The six columns of ex-Service men and women come marching up to form the fourth side of the square. After the service, I will describe their march past and we shall hear the old marching tunes again.

But, for now, the music has stopped. It is 10.56 exactly. The Choir of the Chapels Royal, in their Tudor costumes of scarlet and gold, have taken their places on the near side of the Cenotaph. Now the High Commissioners of Commonwealth countries, some a little hesitant but deftly ushered into position, come out of the Home Office building to form four groups round the Cenotaph. Each carries a wreath of red poppies. The picture is completed by members of the Cabinet and leaders of the Opposition.

We remember one and three quarter million men and women from Britain and the Commonwealth who gave their lives. Shoulder to shoulder in a single rank they would stretch some five hundred miles from the Cenotaph, up England and over the Scottish border, to the outskirts of Aberdeen. A sobering statistic: the sum total of a nation's grief.

Earlier we had heard that wistful little tune *Isle of Beauty*, played each year since the very first Armistice Day service in 1919, round a temporary Cenotaph made of wood. Dedicated to this 'green and pleasant land', for which so many died, it seems like a heartcry from the dead. I quoted the words in 1984:

'Tis the hour when happy faces
Shine amidst our tapers light.
Who will fill our vacant places?
Who will sing our songs tonight?
Thro' the mist that floats above us
Softly sounds the vesper bell
Like a voice from those that love us
Isle of Beauty, fare thee well.

It is 10.59. Her Majesty the Queen leaves through the doorway opposite, between two ranks of Queen's Scouts. My eye darts between my stop-watch and the scene before me. I quote the Order of Service which ends, 'We pray for Peace, and that we may be worthy of the sacrifice made on our behalf'. I stop talking. It is exactly thirty seconds to 11 o'clock. All other BBC services and every local station join the main transmission. At twenty-two seconds to eleven, the chimes of Big Ben start to echo down Whitehall followed by the first stroke of eleven o'clock. The Two Minutes' Silence begins.

"At the going down of the sun and in the morning, we will remember them."

The Silence is broken only by the cry of a child hoisted on a father's shoulder and by the distant rumble of traffic, reminding us that we don't all stop as we used to do. It is followed by the Last Post, sounded by twelve buglers of the Royal Marines.

The Queen, wearing a black coat and hat, and with a black handbag over her left arm, stands quite alone, the Royal Princes behind her. There is no bodyguard, no bullet-proof glass. We don't do things that way. As she steps forward to lay her wreath, she does so as Head of State and on behalf of the nation. The row of politicians await their turn. In one glance, we see a democratic Government under a constitutional monarchy, paying homage to those who died to keep it so.

I use a diagram to describe the scene (page 94). On it, the position is noted of each of some fifty-seven wreaths of poppies which, in a few minutes, will turn the white stone base of the Cenotaph a vivid scarlet. First the Royal wreaths, then the Government and Opposition leaders', followed by the High Commissioners'; the evolution of Empire to Commonwealth. Finally, wreaths are laid by the Chiefs of Staff on behalf of the three Services. From a window, the Queen Mother, who lost a brother in the first War, watches with other lady members of the Royal Family.

I keep my commentary a little ahead of what is actually taking place, to give details of the service which follows as soon as the final wreaths are laid on behalf of the civilian services, the Merchant Navy and Fishing Fleet, and the Merchant Air Services.

"The next voice you will hear will be that of the Bishop of London." The service is quite short. It always contains the hymn *O God, our help in ages past*. Twelve trumpeters of the Royal Air Force sound *Reveillé* and the great gathering in Whitehall sings the National Anthem.

While the Queen and other members of the Royal Family leave Whitehall, we look back forty years through the eyes of Frank Gillard, a BBC War Correspondent during the invasion of Normandy. In a recording, he speaks vividly of the organised chaos of the D-Day beaches and of the eventual liberation of Europe. I had listened to his voice forty years before, out in the Far East.

But now it is 1984, in London, and the veterans of two World Wars are about to March past the Cenotaph. I have timed both verse and chorus of each of the old songs we are about to hear. My aim is to describe the scene over the

Left: *Remembrance Service at the Cenotaph, Whitehall.*

verse and leave the chorus to speak for itself. It is the words of the chorus that people know and love.

One of my two stopwatches is set back to zero and I keep a careful eye on it. 'Quick March' is the order as I start the watch but the pace, in fact, is slow, just one hundred paces to the minute, in deference to advancing years. Six abreast they come, medals across their chests, poppies in their buttonholes – heads greying now, but held high, with shoulders back, and pride in their hearts. So flows the human tide of service to the nation. They are led by members of the Executive Council of the Legion, each with a rolled umbrella in his right hand and wearing that uniquely British badge of authority, the Bowler Hat.

*It's a long way to Tipperary* – and quite far enough, too, down to Parliament Square, when you are eighty-five years old. There, the statue of Sir Winston Churchill surveys the scene, reminding us of the days when we, in these islands, stood alone for freedom.

And still they come, in an endless column: men of the Eighth Army, the Desert Rats – holders of the Military Medal, the Chindits, the Burma Star Association and the blind of St Dunstan's, guided along by friends. The bands play *Pack up your troubles* and *There'll always be an England*.

More wreaths are handed in to be added to those on the Cenotaph and, as the marching feet fade away down Whitehall, the bands play *Wish me luck as you wave me Goodbye*.

On occasions such as this, broadcasting is the instrument of national unity, shared by expatriates throughout the world. It is always a moving experience and an honour to take part.

To end the broadcast in 1984, my twenty-first and last on Remembrance Sunday, I recall the message scrawled on a rock at Kohima:

> When you go home, tell them of us and say
> For your tomorrow, we gave our today.

# CHAPTER 12
# Prince Charles gets Married

"We have to get the rough stuff seated by ten o'clock." The clipped tones of the Guards Officer had a ring of authority. He was, after all, a senior usher at the wedding of a lifetime. "Until they're all seated," he added by way of explanation, "we can't take the polythene sheet off the carpet". One had visions of the 'rough stuff'. Those agonising decisions about the (compulsory) hat, the new dress, the colour scheme, uniforms to be cleaned, medals polished, morning dress to be hired from Moss Bros.

At nine o'clock, two thousand of the best dressed people in Britain, clutching their precious invitations, would start flooding in to fill the nave of St Paul's. They would wear the satisfied expressions of people in the right place at the right time. Little did they know they were the 'rough stuff'!

"Crowned heads in the Quire, family and V.I.P.s under the Dome – here's the seating plan," and the Guards Officer marched off to deploy a small army of more junior ushers.

We were talking early in the morning of 29th July, 1981. Nobody had ever seen a Prince of Wales get married. The last time it had happened was on the 10th March, 1863, at St George's Chapel, Windsor. Queen Victoria, still in mourning for Prince Albert, had watched from a gallery and shed a few tears as the future King Edward VII married Princess Alexandra. Now, 118 years later, an historic moment was to be broadcast and televised to a world-wide audience.

Planning had begun as soon as the engagement of the Prince of Wales to Lady Diana Spencer was announced. St Paul's was chosen because it is bigger than Westminster Abbey, so more guests could be invited. Also, the route from Buckingham Palace is longer, so more people would see the processions.

It was to be a national celebration. Everyone loves a wedding and this was to be the biggest and best. Even the BBC's heart beat a little faster. Cliff Morgan, Head of Television Outside Broadcasts, was a happy man: "Wimbledon and the

Open Golf will be out of the way and it doesn't clash with a Test match – July 29th couldn't be better". Just as well, because sixty cameras from all over Britain would be deployed in St Paul's and along the route. Radio, too, had a grand design, with eight commentary positions, in addition to mine in St Paul's. Welshmen were much in evidence, with Wynford Vaughan-Thomas at Buckingham Palace, Alun Williams in Trafalgar Square, Peter Jones in Fleet Street and, a masterstroke, Richard Burton to present the whole programme from the studio in Broadcasting House. I felt honoured, as an Englishman, to have prime position.

The bride was 'represented' in our team, by Sue Macgregor in the Strand, Susannah Simons at Clarence House, with a first view of the Wedding Dress, and slightly to my surprise, by Lorraine Chase, the Eliza Doolittle of *Pygmalion*, near Temple Bar. Rolf Harris, to represent the Commonwealth, was to be at Australia House, with assorted children, while Prudence Glyn, the fashion expert, was to join Brian Johnston on the Queen Anne Memorial outside St Paul's to watch the guests going in. Terry Wogan, in the Mall, would set the ball rolling at 7.30 am on Radio 2; Radio 4 would join in at 9.45 and the World Service with a huge audience at 10.10.

Some of the all-star cast had little experience of live outside broadcasting and my guess was that they would find it difficult. I felt we had too many of them and that the producer might get verbal indigestion trying to fit them all in. The Military and the Milliners were among the first to leap into action.

I visited my friends the Welsh Guards. "Guard of Honour at the Palace," said the Adjutant with satisfaction, "we expected it of course, but it's nice to know for sure".

"I shall ride to the left of the coach" – this was the Squadron Corporal Major of the Life Guards speaking – "and the major will be on the right. Can't remember when we last did a Prince of Wales Escort – must have been in 1969 at the Investiture in Caernarvon – one officer and thirty-seven other ranks I think it is", and he hurried off to check. "Of course" – over his shoulder – "we shall need 170 horses altogether, with the Sovereign's Escort as well." Naturally – no trouble at all.

At London district HQ, in Whitehall, the logistics and timings were taking shape. A wall map showed how the route would be lined by 92 officers and 1,826 other ranks, and where each of ten bands would be stationed – a sort of four-mile musical relay race. "Clicking into place quite nicely," said the Staff Officer, putting another pin in the map to make sure.

The police and the souvenir industry were also busy; the former searching every room overlooking the route, the latter creating a vast quantity of authorised and non-authorised bric-a-brac. Fashion writers, photographers, cake, mug and flag makers, not to mention fireworks experts, all had a field day.

For my part, I turned my attention to St Paul's, from which I had broadcast the funeral of Sir Winston Churchill in 1965, the Silver Jubilee in 1977, and many other services on special occasions – but never a Royal Wedding. There had never been one there.

As soon as a draft Order of Service was available, I asked the sacrist, the Reverend Michael Moxon, to take me through it in detail, and the organist, Christopher Dearnley, to play over the music on the piano in his flat and tell me its derivation and the reasons for its choice; Prince Charles had apparently taken a personal interest in this.

Down in the Crypt, our BBC radio engineers were preparing to give sound to the world; not only to our radio and television service but to ITV and seventy-one other countries as well. The formidable trio of American networks, ABC, NBC and CBS, were present in force along the route with their own cameras. But from within St Paul's all their sound and vision came from the BBC. In this way, the number of the microphones was reduced to fifty-five, slung across the nave, hiding behind the altar plate, buried among the flowers and perched in the Whispering Gallery. Seven and a half miles of cable linked them to the control point below.

The wedding was to be a considerable musical occasion, and the co-ordination of organ, orchestra, Bach Choir, the Choir of St Paul's and the Chapels Royal, the soloists and the trumpeters, all playing and singing in different parts of the Cathedral, would require expertise and careful rehearsal, not only by the musicians, but by our engineers as well. Harold Kutscherauer deserved a medal for the sound balance he achieved that day.

A week before the Wedding, an unexpected summons reached me from

Buckingham Palace, to attend what was described as a 'briefing' for television and radio. A puzzled quorum of well-known faces and names gathered in the office of John Haslam, the Deputy Press Secretary, an old friend and a former member of my department of the BBC. These included Tom Fleming and Angela Rippon, batting for the BBC, and the ITV team of Alastair Burnett, Andrew Gardiner and Judith Chalmers. Much to our astonishment we were then ushered into the presence of the Prince of Wales and Lady Diana – as she was then.

What was actually said is strictly speaking 'off the record', but I doubt if I am betraying a state secret by revealing that we were received with much cordiality, and a trolley of drinks, in a medium-sized sitting room. They had apparently thought it a good idea to meet the people who were going to describe "our great day". How nice – and how kind.

Prince Charles was deeply concerned, worried about what best to do with all the wedding presents, and which of thousands of invitations to accept – "we go where we can do most good".

Lady Diana, trying not to look too tall, stood slightly askew and looked us straight in the eyes. I found her very helpful. It would, she thought, take about three and a half minutes to walk up the aisle at the start (it did) and yes, the wedding dress was lovely. I asked Prince Charles if he would set a slow pace back to the West Door at the end. He cheerfully agreed.

Slightly bemused, we made our way back across the Palace Courtyard. I was frankly delighted by this unexpected meeting with our supposed future King and Queen and resolved to do my part that little bit better than ever before.

It took three weeks to 'rig' St Paul's for sound and vision. For the last three days before the Wedding, the Cathedral was closed to the public, but the two weeks or so prior to that produced a diverting head-on collision between broadcasters, workmen and public.

The dais, where the actual ceremony was to take place, was about sixteen feet by ten feet, and a stout American lady took an early opportunity to stand on it. "Say, is this where her blood turns blue?" An engineer, suspending a microphone above her head, reassured her on that point. "OK, Elmer, take it now, honey." Elmer, festooned with cameras, took aim and a Christmas card was born – "Gee, wait till I show them back home".

*Wedding of Prince Charles and Lady Diana Spencer, 29th July 1981.*

Elsewhere, twenty-four television cameras (twelve each for BBC and ITV) were being ineffectually disguised as cardboard pillars. Chattering groups of tourists, their cameras red hot with frantic photography, mingled with sound engineers and lighting experts. The triforium became a mass of cables as banks of lights were hauled up eighty feet and installed along the sides of the nave. A vast crane appeared outside to hoist a camera to the top of the dome for that dramatic downward shot. Michael Lumley, the senior TV producer, surveyed a battery of some thirty screens in his control van parked outside. It was he who decided what you saw that day.

Sixty feet up in the West Gallery, my commentary box resembled an airless semi-detached rabbit hutch. Next door to me was Tom Fleming in TV's rather more spacious apartment. I arranged for better soundproofing between us and the installation of an electric fan: otherwise there might have been a Funeral as well as a Wedding.

The great day was a Wednesday. On the Sunday before, early in the morning, the carriage procession trundled down the route to St Paul's – best horses, but second-best uniforms. The concertina-like steps of the glass coach were unwound by a footman, and a stand-in male Bride walked quickly up the steps while the State Trumpeters deafened him with a 39-second fanfare.

Each procession came separately, supervised by Sir John Miller, the Crown Equerry. Guards officers, disguised in bowler hats, and carrying rolled umbrellas on a cloudless day, checked the troops lining the streets, while the Guard of Honour from the three Services presented arms to an imaginary Sovereign.

Brian Johnston came to St Paul's to interview me for *Down Your Way*. My choice of music was *God Bless the Prince of Wales*, which had been elbowed out of the Wedding Ceremony, naturally enough, by the National Anthem. But it is an excellent tune, rarely heard, and surely appropriate on this occasion.

Rehearsals inside were on the Monday and Tuesday. The trouble is that they always take place in mufti – and without the principal players. Imagination of a high order is needed to visualise the scene as it will look on the day. Who would think, for example, that the middle-aged gentleman, with a placard round his neck marked 'Earl of Ulster', was really representing a little boy of six? Princess Margaret had become a stout gentleman with glasses. It was all most confusing.

Clothes, colours and timing must not take the commentator by surprise. The cheerful ladies of the Bach Choir would, I was told, wear white blouses and black skirts. The Dean and Chapter would emerge in copes of red, silver and gold. Kiri Te Kanawa – not then a Dame – whose lovely voice would rise like a lark up to the Dome – revealed that she would wear a green hat and would not kiss anyone for fear of catching a cold – a pity.

The State Trumpeters, sober-suited now, will appear resplendent in their gold-lace uniforms and velvet caps. The Trumpeters from the Royal Military School of Music at Kneller Hall tell me exactly when they will lift their trumpets to their lips during Parry's great anthem *I was glad*. They identify a quiet thirty-second period, suitable for commentary, when the Prince and Princess – as she will be by then – move up to the Altar.

I find the Dean was at school with me, which helps. We walk from the dais, stop-watch in hand, to the south aisle, where the Register will be signed. He introduces me to Sir John Betjeman, the Poet Laureate, in a wheelchair, who wishes me luck; "the words are so important," he says.

Finally, the National Anthem, specially arranged by Sir David Willcocks for orchestra, organ, cathedral choir, Bach Choir and trumpeters is rehearsed. It is spellbinding – a knockout. The BBC and ITV technicians, still crawling about the Cathedral, stop work and applaud, something I have never known to happen before. They are a hard-bitten lot, used to the best; but this is special.

A charming lady represents the Bride. She has brought with her some long curtains which are attached to her shoulders with safety pins. They represent the train of the dress, its length still a state secret.

Now, with her temporary husband, she breaks the world record back to the West Door. I stare at my stop watch in disbelief: three minutes two seconds. Elgar's *Pomp and Circumstance March No. 4*, which will accompany them down the aisle, lasts for five and a quarter minutes. My hope is that the Prince and Princess would take about four and a half, leaving forty-five seconds of the rousing crescendo to take them outside into public view. After all, he had promised... but how slow is 'slowly'?

My aim had been to describe this glittering climax in two parts, with a musical 'bridge' in the middle. Now I had my doubts. Preoccupied, I overshoot Oxford Circus on the tube, and have to walk back to Broadcasting House from Bond Street.

Here I find the full radio cast assembled for a briefing by the producer, Patricia Ewing, later to be Controller of Radio 5. I speak to Richard Burton, encased in a neck support, which will not make life any easier for him in the studio. He is affable and helpful. We have a mutual problem. How long would the 'titivating' take when the Bride arrives at the West Door? The Emanuels, designers of the dress, would aim at one and a half minutes (in the event it was one minute and twenty five seconds). Would Richard please restrict his cue to thirty seconds, to give time to build up the scene? He would, and did - exactly.

A word too with Terry Wogan, with whom I had launched 'Wogan's Winner' some years before. I suggest potentially productive questions he might ask me during our 'two-way' encounter on the following morning. I did the same with John Timpson, an old friend of Royal Tours, who I was to meet on the *Today* programme.

Then to my hotel, next to Broadcasting House, and a final appraisal of my notes. The alarm call came at 4.30 am, but I had already been up for an hour, fortified by cups of tea while wrestling my final peroration into shape; red brackets meant 'omit', in the event of a sprint down the nave, and green brackets meant 'add', if the pace was slower than expected.

Finally satisfied, the notes are stuck on cardboard and my briefcase equipped with stop-watch, binoculars, coffee and chocolate. Then on with the morning dress and downstairs to board the waiting bus. But first Rolf Harris, a keen photographer, takes a photograph of me with Brian Johnston and Alun Williams. An odd thing to happen at 5.30 am: that picture still stands on my desk today.

Despite the early hour, we are a jolly crowd in the bus, touring the broadcasting positions and dropping a member of our team off at his or her appointed place with cries of "good luck". Lorraine Chase wears a red hat with a wide brim which narrowly avoids Brian Johnston's eye. Rolf Harris has brought his guitar, and Peter Baxter has taken a day off from cricket to help me in St Paul's. Soon we are eating BBC sausages in the car park. At half past six, our briefcases searched for bombs, we go inside to greet our engineers in the Crypt. From there, Peter Hunt, an old friend, is connected to me, up in the West Gallery, by a cue-light signalling system. On him will depend the technical balance of my commentary with the speech and singing of the Wedding. We go through the Service in detail; I warn him when to expect the cue-light signals.

Then, upstairs from the Crypt to the empty Cathedral; at least almost empty. A man is spraying the flowers with water, the organ tuner is tuning the organ with one finger and there is a lady busy with mop and pail. I felt she had a big job.

Armed with the seating plans, I make a careful check of the two rows of four crimson and gold chairs, on either side of the dais, where the Queen and Prince Philip and senior members of the Royal and Spencer families will sit. One of a team of seven labradors is sniffing for explosives; he sticks his nose into my briefcase and I give him a piece of chocolate. Diplomacy and protocol are nicely blended in the seating arrangements; reigning monarchs in the Quire and ten Presidents under the Dome. Our own Prime Minister, Mrs Thatcher, can only achieve the eleventh row, while five ex-Prime Ministers are three rows further back. Mrs Reagan sits near the President of France, M. Mitterand, and I wonder whether her French will stand the test. In front of her is the President of Zimbabwe, whose name is Banana. The King of Tonga has a specially reinforced chair; at twenty-six stone, he is on the heavy side.

A fourteen-page document arrives from Buckingham Palace with details of dresses and uniforms. Mysterious stuff for two males sixty feet up in a small box at 7.30 am. What is one to make of 'floating panels cascading from the yoke'? I settle for colours only and later award first prize to Mrs Shand Kydd, so elegant in blue.

At 8.12, my date is kept with John Timpson, apparently on the move in a radio car down the Mall. We persuade the organ tuner to desist until we finish. Then time seems to fly.

The organisation is perfect. Dignity and precision go hand in hand as each piece of a breathtaking jigsaw is fitted effortlessly into place. I talk about it all to Terry Wogan on Radio 2. The 'Rough Stuff' are all present by ten o'clock and the polythene sheet is removed to reveal the red carpet in all its 697 feet of glory. Kidderminster would be proud of it. I look down on the new hats: a spectrum of blues, reds and yellows. A milliner's dream.

It is 10.20. Here come the Yeomen of the Guard in their round Tudor hats and the Gentlemen at Arms in silver helmets. They make a brilliant scarlet border to the scene, as the eight crowned heads take their places in the Quire. At 10.32 exactly, the Dean and Chapter move to the West Door to greet, first, the Lord Mayor of London at 10.36, then the Queen and the Royal Family at 10.42 and finally, in Naval uniform, the Royal Bridegroom, looking as nervous as any other.

Meanwhile the World Service, with its millions of extra listeners, has joined the domestic services. In three minutes I draw their eyes, in their imagination, up the rich red carpet to the vista of the Dome and to the little dais beneath it, bordered by lilies, hydrangeas and roses, then to the dark oak choir stalls with their yellow lamps, and on to the white altar beyond, with its great marble canopy above. I hope they get the picture.

Now for the Bride. The fanfare echoes away outside and, on my monitor screen, I see the long white train of the wedding dress trailing down the steps as Richard Burton, from the studio, sends her on her way with a pre-arranged cue to me – "Go, lovely rose, how sweet and fair she seems to be". I compare Lady Diana – to her considerable advantage – with Catherine of Aragon who, 480 years before, had come from Spain to the old cathedral to marry the young Prince Arthur, Prince of Wales. She wore a hooped skirt called a farthingale. "Now, below, in a beautiful dress of creamy silk taffeta, is her modern counterpart, a young and delightful bride of poise and style and dignity – but one born and bred in the rolling acres of England's countryside."

I watch for the signal from the Sacrist and stop talking just in time, as the organ crashes in with the *Trumpet Voluntary*, and the bridal procession moves up the nave. The world smiles indulgently at nervous mistakes. Lady Diana Spencer marries Philip Charles and he promises to share her worldly goods. Nevertheless, the Archbishop of Canterbury, Dr Runcie, declares them man and wife to an enormous cheer from the crowds listening to the relayed service outside.

The youngest of the four bridesmaids is Clementine Hambro, aged five, a great grand-daughter of Sir Winston Churchill. She sits, sucking her thumb in contemplative mood, on the same spot where her great grandfather's coffin had lain at his State Funeral in 1965, eleven years before she was born.

Finally, the Service, with its magnificent music, stirring hymns and glorious singing, and with the Lesson read by the Speaker and the Address given by the Archbishop of Canterbury, draws to a close. After the National Anthem, the emotion is almost tangible.

For me, all had gone well so far. But now to the climax as they come back down the 'river of red carpet' to the East Door (at, I am glad to say, exactly the right pace).

And so outside to tumultuous cheers all the way back to Buckingham Palace and more still when they come out on the balcony for the famous kiss.


No other nation on earth could have drawn on such history and heritage, nor summoned up such expertise and experience, to stage a Wedding like this. At the time, it seemed a fairy tale come true, displayed to the world with rich ceremonial and classic dignity. It had been a privilege to play a part, among so many striving for perfection, on an unique day in our lifetime.

And the Rough Stuff? They loved it.

# CHAPTER 13
# The Train at Platform Two

Victoria Station has been embellished with flowers and Romanian flags, a red carpet has been laid on Platform Two, press photographers, television cameramen and radio commentators are in position. Now all depends on the engine driver.

It is the State Visit of His Excellency the President of the Socialist Republic of Romania and Madame Elena Ceausescu. The date is 1st June 1978. Twelve years later they will both be shot by their own countrymen. But for now, London is at their feet. A line of dignitaries, in uniform or morning dress, stand ready on the platform; among them the Prime Minister, the Foreign Secretary, the Lord Mayors of London and of Westminster, the Commissioner of Police and the Chiefs of Staff of the three Services. Her Majesty the Queen, Prince Philip and other members of the Royal Family are in the Royal Waiting Room which adjoins the platform. They will emerge as the train enters the station.

Normally the Queen's subjects are presented to her. Now, the roles are reversed. Her Majesty, unless my eyes are deceiving me, holds a small card in the palm of her hand with the names of the reception party on it. It behoves them to stand in the right order.

*Queen Elizabeth and President Nicolae Ceausescu, Victoria Station, 1978.*

The engine driver, having brought the train from Gatwick Airport, must feel a touch of nerves when approaching Battersea Power Station. In front of him stretches the bridge over the Thames and then the downward curve into the station. He has two objectives: to arrive at exactly the right time (always 12.30), and in the right place. He is unlikely to miss Platform Two or, being a highly experienced driver, to run into the buffers. He must, however, contrive to bring the train to a stop when the carriage door from which the President and his wife will appear is exactly opposite the red carpet. Here the Queen will be standing to greet her guests. In my experience, these twin goals are invariably achieved with absolute precision.

The side entrance to Victoria Station is not one of the more beautiful parts of London – but one has to start somewhere. Things can only get better.

A superb Guard of Honour of the Grenadier Guards adds sparkle to the drab surroundings. President de Gaulle, on his State Visit (and each Head of State makes only one of these), was visibly impressed. His reaction was clearly picked up on our 'effects' microphone, just above his head. As he stood, quite alone, to take the salute, we heard one word – "Magnifique!"

These arrival ceremonies would usually be broadcast on the BBC World Service. One commentary position would be on the platform inside the station, and the other on the roof of the Continental Ticket Office which used to be outside in Hudson's Place, an appropriate name in my case. Access was by ladder and it afforded an excellent view over the bearskin caps of the Guard of Honour. The officer in command has the unenviable task of reporting the Guard ready for inspection in the language of the visiting Head of State; not too difficult in French, perhaps, but much more so in Romanian. This achieved, the visitor then inspects the Guard, accompanied by Prince Philip, while the band plays a medley of tunes and I tell listeners something about him and about the programme which lies ahead for the next four days. State Visits always begin on Tuesdays and end on Fridays.

Open carriages are then brought up and London's traffic prepares to be disrupted. Buckingham Palace is only a few hundred yards from Victoria Station: too short a distance for the Head of State to see or be seen. Hence a longer route, lined by troops and bedecked with flags, is cordoned off to normal traffic, causing harsh words to be said by motorists. However, the lunch hour for London's typists, munching sandwiches in the coffee bars, and for senior civil servants on the way to their clubs, is brightened for a few moments. The Sovereign's Escort of Household Cavalry, always a stirring sight, clatters down Victoria Street through Parliament Square, down Whitehall and the Mall to Buckingham Palace. The Queen rides with the Visiting Head of State; Prince Philip with the Head of State's wife or husband.

*A warm welcome outside Buckingham Palace for President Ceausescu of Romania.*

The crowds are disappointingly small and largely indifferent; many will have no idea who the visitor is unless he is the President of the United States. The contrast with a State Visit made by the Queen overseas is most marked. I remember standing with my wife in a cheering crowd on the pavement outside the Opera House in Paris, while on our honeymoon in 1957, when the Queen and the President of France came out on the balcony.

Some arrivals have taken place at Windsor where an impressive 'Rank-Past' of Household Cavalry, and sometimes also of the King's Troop, Royal Horse Artillery, would be held in the Castle Quadrangle. Our viewpoint for this was a small storeroom near St George's Hall, which was gutted by the calamitous fire of November 1992. On these occasions, a pavilion was erected at the end of the Royal Mile, where greetings could conveniently take place and the Guard of Honour be inspected.

The President of Malawi fell foul of a strike by Air Traffic Controllers in Holland, while en route to Britain. A former Comptroller of the Lord Chamberlain's Office described to me, in an interview, how the Guard of Honour 'piled arms' in a scene reminiscent of the Crimean War. The horses munched the grass and the Cabinet held an impromptu meeting behind the pavilion. Order was restored when the President eventually arrived forty-five minutes late.

In more recent times the President of Poland, a former shipyard electrician from Gdansk, was greeted at Windsor. He must have reflected on the ups and downs of life as he rode, with the Queen, up the Royal Mile to the Castle, accompanied by a magnificent escort of Household Cavalry. He had certainly not come to mend the fuses.

State Visits follow set lines to guarantee equal treatment to all Heads of State. The first afternoon will normally include visits to the Tomb of the Unknown Warrior in Westminster Abbey, to St James's Palace to receive an Address of Welcome and finally, to the Queen Mother at Clarence House. But the focus of the first day will be on the State Banquet at Buckingham Palace.

This is a formal and 'public' occasion. Britain is entertaining Romania. It is an International Match and speeches by the Queen and her guest are broadcast to the world via the BBC's best silver-gilt Royal microphones. The press can preview the scene in the Ballroom, where the Banquet is held, but they are not invited to attend it.

The seating plan is folded inside the menu card. This reveals a total of about a hundred and seventy guests, with only ten at the top table, including the Archbishop of Canterbury to say Grace. Everyone else, including some members of the Royal Family, sit on either side of two long tables. Here you will find Cabinet Ministers, captains of industry, Lord Mayors, diplomats, judges, military men and even a token trade unionist; white tie and tails for the men and new long evening dresses for the ladies. Decorations are worn. If you are invited, you have certainly 'arrived'.

It is also a sight to dazzle the eye and one, incidentally, which has been closely inspected by the Queen late that afternoon. Gold plate gleams on the walls and sideboards while, on the tables covered by white tablecloths, candles flicker on the gold candelabra, plates of silver gilt glint under the lights and gold cutlery is the order of the day. On the other side of the Atlantic – I will not be more specific – Prince Philip, so it is said, was advised "to keep your fork, Dook, there's pie after". This doesn't normally happen at Buckingham Palace.

In front of the Queen and President Ceausescu is a circular dish made of silver gilt, embossed with flowers and animals. At its centre a Gothic Rose with the Crown and Cypher of Queen Anne and Charles the Second. Our microphones blend nicely with the decor: I feel proud of them. Their cables end up in the capable hands of our engineers in a room behind the Musicians' Gallery. Here, a Guards Band plays a selection of music which, it is hoped, will be to the liking of the chief guests.

President Giscard d'Estaing of France and his wife no doubt felt at home with *Rue de la Paix*, *A la Can-Can* and *Moulin Rouge*. On the other hand, Queen Beatrix of the Netherlands, in 1982, might have expected *Tulips in Amsterdam*, but instead got *Colonel Bogey*, *Mary Poppins* and *HMS Pinafore*!

It all not only looks and sounds good, but also smells like a flower shop. Large floral arrangements, at two corners, augment those on the tables and also serve to conceal amber and green 'traffic lights', operated by the Chief Steward, who stands behind the Queen. Amber is the signal to take post at the serving stations and green either to clear away or serve the next course. This is done by the footmen, in their eighteenth-century style scarlet uniforms, decorated with gold braid. They wear scarlet plush knee breeches, pink stockings and black buckle shoes and make a vivid living border to a glittering scene.

The menu is written in French. I believe Mr Egon Ronay thinks it should be written in English. Occasionally there is a compromise. The President of France, for example, was offered 'Selle d'Agneau Windsor'. The food seems to have decreased over the years. It has settled down at four courses – less, I think, than most people would expect – but with suitable wine accompanying each. Sherry will be served with the Consommé Madrilène, a German white wine with the Suprème de Saumon, Chateau Latour with the Saddle of Lamb and champagne with the Bombe Glacée Royale. And of course port and brandy to follow; not to mention the Pipers of the Scots Guards marching round the room. Some find this hard to take.

A problem arises when the visiting Head of State does not speak English, as in the case of President Ceausescu. This is neatly solved by placing a translation of his speech in front of each guest. During the meal an interpreter, already fed, sits behind the Queen and the President to relay whatever they have to say to each other. When the time comes for the speeches, the microphones, mute until then to avoid Royal and Presidential chit-chat being overheard, are switched on by the Queen herself. The speeches are recorded at Bush House and broadcast a little later on the World Service, with the addition of a 'scene-set'. Facilities are also arranged by the BBC for broadcasters from the visiting country.

At Windsor Castle some 150 people sit on either side of one immense table in St George's Hall. It is 160 feet long and wide enough for three people to sit at each end. The only way to lay it is to walk down the middle in stockinged feet with a ruler; otherwise you end up with half a dozen places left, but no table to lay them on. The finished article with its candelabra, flowers and gold plate is a breathtaking sight.

The State Visit is now well and truly launched, but much eating remains to be done. A banquet at the Guildhall, given by the Lord Mayor of London on the Wednesday, rivals Buckingham Palace in splendour. On the Thursday, it is the turn of the visitor to entertain the Queen at Claridges Hotel. Between these gastronomic occasions, there will be talks, lunch with the Prime Minister at 10 Downing Street and visits from the leaders of other political parties.

Most of the King of Sweden's visit in 1975 took place in Scotland and all Heads of State have, as it were, an 'awayday'. President Ceausescu went to British Aerospace at Filton. Earlier, his wife had visited the Royal Institute of Chemistry, in which subject she apparently had a Romanian equivalent of an 'A' level.

Except in Britain, being Head of State seems to be a transient occupation.

After describing a succession of visitors, over the years, stepping from the train at Victoria Station, or from a car at Windsor, I am struck by the enviable permanence and stability of the British monarchy.

Elsewhere, Kings may be exiled, Presidents overthrown, or come to the end of their terms. Revolutions take their toll in various ways. Fortunately, those who walk in procession with the Queen and Prince Philip to the elegant splendour of the Ballroom at Buckingham Palace for a State Banquet do not normally end up facing a firing squad. Her Majesty does not, one imagines, expect her guests to be shot.

The President of Romania and Madame Elena Ceaucescu had given the Queen a carpet. An exchange of presents is obligatory. The Queen gave the President a hunting rifle. Perhaps that was prophetic.

# CHAPTER 14
# A Sporting Life

The King lowered his binoculars and turned away.

I will never forget the look of disappointment on his face.

It was 1942: wartime. The Derby was run on the July course at Newmarket and King George's horse, Big Game, after being up with the leaders, had faded in the final two furlongs. It must have been a bitter pill for the King to swallow.

My artillery battery was under canvas near Cambridge. Petrol was scarce

*Grand National, 29th March 1969. Kilburn falls with his jockey, T. Carberry.*

and no military vehicle could be used to reach the course. With another young officer, I managed to get a lift to Newmarket, passing, en route, our Battery Commander, head into the wind, gamely pedalling down that long straight road. It was my introduction to Racing.

Later, in Malaya, after the Japanese surrender in 1945, I had a brief, successful, but sad, career as an owner. The Army got racing restarted with commendable speed and I became the temporary joint owner of a horse called Vintage. In its first race it was beaten by a short head, but in its second, at Kuala Lumpur, it romped home by five lengths. With the proceeds of our victory, we held a dance in the Officers' Mess and drank a toast to the gallant animal. Sadly, it died that night, apparently suffering from an ulcer which was probably due to inadequate food during the Japanese occupation.

My next encounter with the Sport of Kings was at Aintree in 1955 when, as Senior Outside Broadcasts Producer for the BBC in the North, it fell to me to organise radio coverage of the Grand National. Negotiations took place with the redoubtable Mrs Mirabelle Topham, who lived on the course at Paddock Lodge, and success was rewarded by a glass of the best sherry.

Some years earlier, Mrs Topham had engaged her own commentators, who fell far short of professional standards. The BBC was restored to favour on condition that, to preserve her copyright, the commentary was recorded on tape exactly one second before transmission to the world.

The arrival of television in the North caused all sorts of fresh problems, but Peter Dimmock eventually persuaded Mrs Topham to sanction the building of a brick tower on the inside of the course at Bechers Brook. On top of this was placed a television camera; a radio commentator was on the floor below, and the engineers were encamped at the bottom. This gave us splendid coverage of the far end of the course, including the Canal Turn and Valentines.

In those days, our principal racing commentator was Raymond Glendenning, who talked faster than any horse could run. Raymond was assisted by Claude Harrison as 'race reader'. Nowadays the commentators are, of course, their own race readers and would not relish advice being whispered into their ears.

Peter O'Sullevan, now the senior TV racing commentator, was often at the twelfth fence, for radio, at Aintree, and Michael O'Hehir would be at Bechers Brook to deliver a high speed commentary in a rich Irish brogue. The short straw was, and is, the first fence, and the place to avoid. Here all the horses are still standing up – and fields were not restricted to forty as they are today. Imagine a cavalry charge of nearly sixty horses bearing down on you. In a matter of seconds you have to identify both the leaders and the fallers, as well as mentioning as many others as possible. Everyone wants to know about *their* horse. A daunting task.

Peter Bromley became the BBC's first Racing Correspondent in 1959 and has since described over six thousand races without ever getting the winner wrong. Now, you can't tell a horse's name just by looking at it. It has to have a jockey wearing the owner's colours. Obviously, all the colours are different but the difference is often very slight. If colour blind, don't apply!

Racing commentators live in a world of their own. Racing is too specialised to allow for other activities. Raymond Glendenning was the last of the all-rounders. A deep and up-to-date knowledge of breeding and form, absolute accuracy in recognition, quick wits and a clear voice in a tight finish are the basic requirements. Peter Bromley has all these, to add to unremitting homework, with the aid of cardboard cut-outs of jockeys, painted in the owners' colours. In the 'Commentators' Trade Union', the racing members are held in high regard.

As Head of Radio Outside Broadcasts, I did my best to negotiate advantageous contracts for the BBC with the various sporting authorities. In racing, we wanted access to every racecourse to broadcast any race we chose. The Racecourse Association, for their part, needed regular and accurate information about the day's racing to be broadcast early in the morning. So was born 'Wogan's Winner' on Radio 2, and a racing bulletin containing all the information which racegoers, jockeys and trainers would need. Wogan's Winner didn't often win, but that was really beside the point.

His face was about six inches from the microphone, his eyes unseeing, blood dripping from his nose on to Eamonn Andrews' notes. If ever a boxer was knocked out, this one was. Sympathetic as I was to his predicament, my main concern was that the fight had ended much too soon.

We were nothing if not ambitious in the North, and in the fifties ran a series of live radio boxing broadcasts from the Liverpool Stadium. Raymond Glendenning, or Eamonn Andrews, would usually come up from London and I would meet them at Lime Street station. We would then repair to the Adelphi Hotel for beer and sandwiches and take a taxi to the Stadium.

Our 'slot' on the North of England Home Service was 8.30 to 9.00 pm. Into this half-hour period, a contest of six three-minute rounds, with a minute between each round, would fit neatly – in theory. To achieve this, though, it had to start at 8.33, 'go the distance', and then finish at 8.56. This would give time for a scene-set before the start and a summing-up at the end. Various problems however could, and did, arise. If the previous fight finished early, but not early enough for another one to take place before 8.30, there would be an 'interval', during which the customers were apt to get restive. On the other hand if one of the boxers was stretched out on the canvas at the end of the first round of the broadcast fight, some quick action was required. Providing at least twenty minutes remained it was still possible to get the next fight – a four-rounder – into action and completed before the nine o'clock news. Our expert summariser was Henry Rose, a legendary figure in the world of sporting journalism. "Keep talking, Henry," I would shout, and disappear into the nether regions of the Stadium to contact Johnny Best, the Master of Ceremonies, and urge our reserve pugilists into the ring. Meanwhile the recumbent boxer was being removed with all decent speed!

In view of the possible hazards, you can appreciate why I was anxious that the participants should be durable and well matched – as indeed they usually were.

Boxing produced large audiences for radio because television was not normally allowed live coverage. My negotiations would be with the promoter Harry Levene in his elegant flat near Marble Arch. He would greet me in a silk dressing gown and with a large whisky already poured out. There then ensued a comical game of cat and mouse. I knew perfectly well that Harry wanted the publicity of radio and, not least, the billing in eight million copies of *Radio Times*. On the other hand he wasn't too keen on publicising the broadcast before all the tickets in the Stadium were sold – and he naturally wanted as much money as he could get from the BBC.

A typical encounter would go like this (the figures are hypothetical):

Levene:   Robert, this is the fight of the century. I've paid a fortune to get this boy over here. His manager talks in telephone numbers, and ten of his entourage are staying at the Cumberland Hotel at my expense. I'm doing it for the British Public. How much?

Hudson:   Providing the timing is right, two thousand pounds.

Levene:   (*head in hands*) You must be joking. Do you know what it costs to put on a fight like this? (*Pause*) Three thousand is rock-bottom.

Hudson:   Done.

        (My maximum was four thousand.)

Then we would have another whisky, both well pleased.

*Eamonn Andrews*

The BBC has always had good boxing commentators. Stewart Macpherson rattled on like a machine-gun. Raymond Glendenning and W. Barrington Dalby were a famous pair, although they sometimes read the fight differently from the referee. They were followed by Eamonn Andrews, a good boxer himself, Simon Smith, Desmond Lynam and, in recent times, Ian Darke. Harry Carpenter has held sway on television.

Henry Cooper's fights always drew a large listening audience – thirteen million on at least one occasion. His fight with the then Cassius Clay (Muhammed Ali) had the nation by the ears. Henry is now an accomplished summariser on the radio and the genial Frank Bruno has taken his place in the ring, when not engaged in pantomime. I have no particular liking for boxing myself, but there is no doubt about its popularity on the air.

"If Rugby Union and Rugby League ever got together, football would take a back seat." That was Alan Hardaker, the influential Secretary of the Football League, speaking in the early seventies. We were having lunch at Lytham St Anne's where, for some strange reason, the League have their headquarters. In view of the success of the amateur Rugby Union World Cup and the continued

Right: *World Heavyweight Title Fight. Henry Cooper vs Cassius Clay, 23rd May 1966.*

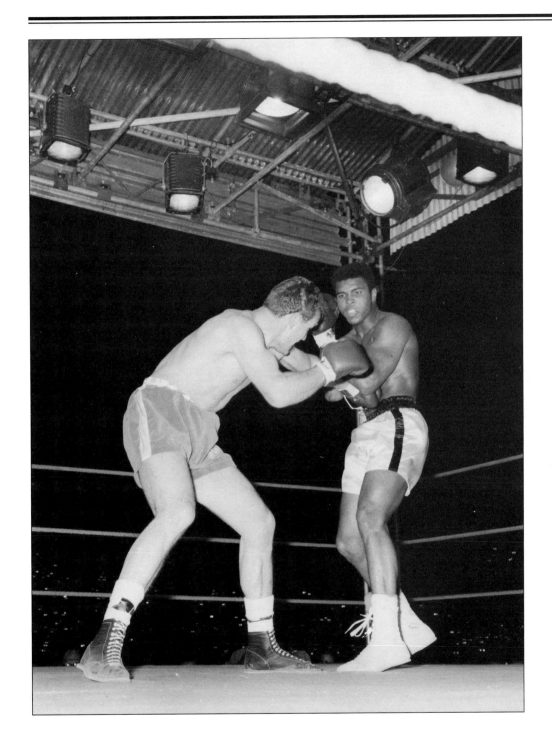

popularity of professional Rugby League in the North, he may well be proved right in the years to come.

It was a congenial lunch, as I had agreed a useful deal for BBC radio and the emerging local stations, which Hardaker was prepared to recommend to the League Management Committee. This august body met at the Great Western Hotel at Paddington. The members seemed to be mostly businessmen, some no doubt very rich, who liked the idea of running a football club. They were not impressive.

Football is a difficult game to broadcast nowadays because of its apparent lack of a coherent pattern. In the old days there was a goalkeeper, two full backs, three half-backs and five forwards, two of whom were 'wingers'; now the talk is of 'back fours', 'sweepers' and 'strikers'. Possibly this is why no

*Wimbledon vs Liverpool at Plough Lane, 14th October 1989.*

commentator on radio has emerged to challenge Alan Clarke and Raymond Glendenning, who broadcast most of the big matches in the fifties and sixties. They painted graphic and accurate pictures of play in the mind of the listener. You could follow the ball with no difficulty. The modern custom of feeding scores from other matches into the commentator's ears, as he is speaking, can only distract him. A radio commentary demands total concentration. In television the problem is solved by superimposing other scores at the bottom of the picture, without disturbing the commentator.

My introduction to football in the North was alarming. Unusually, John Arlott was the commentator. The match was at Preston and the second half was to be broadcast. The first mistake we made was to have lunch in Manchester, which is thirty miles away; the second mistake was to have a bottle of Beaujolais, a 'must' with John in all circumstances. We arrived at Preston by car, after much traffic trouble, just as the referee was blowing his whistle for half-time and the engineer was on the verge of a nervous breakdown. The commentary position was in the front row of the stand and our arrival was greeted with ironic cheers; our neighbours, however, were not averse to describing for us the two goals scored by Preston in the first half. Considering he had seen nothing of the game so far, John made a competent job of the commentary, although he was better at cricket.

Our Northern sports programme, *Sport Spotlight*, aimed to cover those matches not reported earlier by *Sports Report* from London. Angus Mackay, the Sports Editor, seemed to have little idea of geography. The North Region stretched from the Scottish border to a line from Chester to Lincoln. It was a very large area indeed, but Angus's appraisal of time and distance was designed to make all things possible. Somehow, from somewhere, a report would be broadcast in *Sports Report*. We, in the North, had to work the miracle.

Setting up broadcasting points at the grounds, with lines installed by the Post Office, for a one-minute report, was hardly a cost-effective business. Wherever possible we would use the same OB for a report on another sport, for example Rugby League, into our later regional programme.

The alternative was for the football reporter to park his car, with police connivance, ready for a quick getaway; then to make a hectic dash to the nearest 'unattended studio'. Often this would be at least ten miles from the football ground. If you saw a car exceeding the speed limit, at about 4.50pm on a Saturday afternoon, that would be our man. Muttering his report as he drove, his stopwatch ticking on the dashboard, he would hurl himself into the studio, switch himself on the air and breathlessly inform the nation that Blackburn Rovers had won 2 – 1. The star football reporter was Don Davies who had a delightful turn of phrase and was much in demand. Sadly he was killed, along with Henry Rose and many of the Manchester United team in the Munich air disaster of 1958.

*Sport Spotlight* finished each Saturday evening with an item called 'The rest of the Sport', presented, with masterly compression, by Norman Turner. In fact, of course, it was impossible to satisfy all the sporting authorities which exist in Britain.

Regional broadcasting, in those days, gave scope for experiment. In the North we tried describing Bowls, Angling, Cross-Country, Rowing and Sheepdog Trials with varying degrees of success. We always included the Lacrosse results and on one occasion a written report on an Archery contest was delivered to the studio by a taxi driver. Rather to his surprise he found himself ushered to the microphone to make his debut on the air!

In 1966 I described the Opening Ceremony of the World Cup. This immediately preceded the first match of the competition between England and Uruguay, which resulted in a goal-less draw. At that point, I would have laid long odds against England winning the Cup, but they did by 4 – 2 against Germany, and Alan Clarke it was who described the presentation made by the Queen to Bobby Moore, the England captain. The television commentator was Kenneth Wolstenholme, another with roots in the North.

In Lawn Tennis, radio was lucky to have Max Robertson and Fred Perry. Max, the commentator at Wimbledon for forty years, from 1946 to 1986, had remarkable co-ordination of eye and tongue. He spoke very fast, but extremely clearly, and seemed able to keep up with each stroke, even in a men's doubles match. In fact the only criticism of his commentaries came from elderly people for whom he was altogether too much of good thing. The length of a

Lawn Tennis match is indeterminate. Accurate timing is impossible. This has led to flexible 'ball by ball' coverage on both radio and TV. The introduction of the 'tie-break' has helped to reduce the length of a set, but the total duration of the match is still guess work. Rain, too, adds to the problems.

Fred Perry remained loyal to radio and added his prestige and authority, as the only British Wimbledon Singles Champion, to our broadcasts. He has been a good friend of the BBC, who gave him a special eightieth birthday dinner, which I attended at Broadcasting House. So did Dan Maskell, then going strong at eighty-one. The guests of honour were the Duke and Duchess of Kent.

My own contribution to Wimbledon was organisational and social. Coverage from the outside courts was increased by building further commentary positions, at strategic points, which could overlook several courts. This extension was subsequently copied by television. On the social side, the BBC held a cocktail party towards the end of the fortnight, at which Peter Dimmock and I, as Head of Television and Radio Outside Broadcasts, were joint hosts. This was a most congenial occasion, with all the tennis stars attending. One of them, Christine Truman, has since broadcast with our radio team on a regular basis and with much success. Television has two former champions, Virginia Wade and Ann Jones.

Golf has gained much from the expansion of television. Events like the Ryder Cup make compulsive viewing, now that cameras cover almost every hole and the flight of every drive. Radio, too, has expanded its coverage, with 'walkie-talkies' on the course and commentators whispering breathless descriptions of vital putts. In contrast, when Tony Jacklin won the Open at Lytham St Anne's in 1969, radio confined itself to reports from the eighteenth green. It was a memorable moment when Jacklin came striding up the fairway to win for Britain. The amusing and well-informed Henry Longhurst was our radio reporter in the early days. He moved over to television in due course but I doubt if he relished being stuck up a scaffolding tower for hours on end. To my mind, there has been nobody to match Peter Alliss, who is a shining example to other TV commentators.

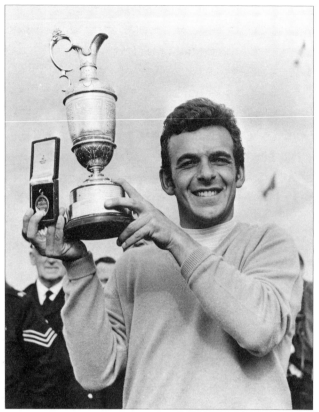

Tom Scott was our leading radio golf reporter for some years and nowadays, a big team is deployed, including Tony Adamson, Chris Rea, who played centre three-quarter for Scotland, and John Fenton, who began his career in the BBC by producing the sound effects for *Take it from Here* and *Much-Binding-in-the-Marsh*. Peter Sellers, starring with Ted Ray in *Ray's a Laugh*, sold John his golf clubs for £25; a transaction successfully concluded in the Gentlemen's cloakroom of the BBC Studio at the Paris Cinema in Lower Regent Street.

*Tony Jacklin with the British Open Championships Trophy at Lytham St Anne's, 12th July 1969.*

In athletics, Harold Abrahams and Rex Alston had run the 100 yards for Cambridge in the 'Varsity Sports of 1923, both of them beating the Oxford pair. Harold went on to win a gold medal in the 1924 Olympics in Paris. Harold and Rex were also a powerful combination for BBC Radio.

Rex, with his incisive voice, described races with clarity and accuracy, while Harold, armed with a battery of stop-watches, supplied every conceivable timing, in addition to expert comment. For such a wonderful athlete, Harold had great humility. He seemed so pleased when I asked him to join the radio team once again for the Olympic Games in Munich in 1972. He was in his seventies then, but as good as ever. Sadly, he died without seeing that splendid film

*Chariots of Fire* which immortalised his gold medal victory.

On television, David Coleman has shown much expertise at the microphone over many years. In the mid-fifties he was working in the BBC Publicity Department in Manchester and I recall inviting him, an excellent athlete himself, to broadcast commentaries on the Police Sports at Park Avenue, Bradford. This he did with much aplomb and went on to fame and fortune. David's brain is so quick that his words don't always match his thoughts – "He's 31 this year – last year he was 30," is an example – not that anyone minds. His exceptional accuracy and speed of thought is perhaps most obvious in the final of the 100 metres, usually won in under ten seconds. Even more impressive is his rapid assimilation of countless names, many foreign, in the earlier heats. The draw for these is often published late on the previous night. The Athletics commentator has much homework to do and needs a quiet single bedroom in which to do it; others of the broadcasting team may have to share.

On three occasions, in the sixties, I was stationed at Chiswick Bridge for the Boat Race, just beyond the finishing post. This was a precaution taken after the launch following the crews and carrying the 'voice of rowing', John Snagge, had broken down. The task of keeping pace with the crews at about 15 mph over the 4 1/4 mile course proved too much for it. The idea was that if all else failed, the chap on the bridge could at least describe the end of the race. Privately, I hoped that the launch would break down again but it never did, although John would hand over to me briefly as the crews approached Barnes Bridge, in order to justify my existence. Many people watched the finish from the banks of the Thames, armed with picnic baskets and transistor radios. I would interview some of them for my scene-set before the race.

When I was a boy the Boat Race had a magical fascination. You were either 'Oxford' or 'Cambridge' and wore a badge to prove it. I was 'Oxford', mainly because my elder brother was there, but in those days Cambridge always seemed to win. More recently, Oxford, with the aid of hefty Americans, seem to have turned the tables.

The Boat Race does not just happen. The river has to be cleared and all other marine traffic stopped. My brother-in-law, when Chairman of the Port of London Authority, had to sanction this; I often wondered what would have happened if he hadn't.

*French champion, Jacques Drion, is partnered in the 110 mile sidecar race by Inge Stoll-Laforge, the first woman ever to compete. TT races, Isle of Man, 1954.*

The Isle of Man, in BBC parlance, was part of the North Region. Apart from Manx cats, it is famous for the TT Races. The roads are closed and the 37-mile course round the island is given over to the motor cyclists. It is a dangerous business, run over ordinary roads with sharp bends, often edged by the stone walls of houses and gardens.

For many years we broadcast the TT Races on a national basis. Often the start was delayed by mist and other programmes were disrupted. Consequently, it became unpopular with the planners. Our broadcasting team centred round the Walker family: Graham, and his son Murray, nowadays in full voice on television. These two had the priceless gift of describing things they couldn't see. Knowing the speed of the machine and every detail of the course, Graham would say, with absolute conviction, "Jones is approaching a long right-hand bend, down the hill – he changes into third gear – and now he should be within your sight, Murray, at Ramsey". And he was! It was uncanny.

George Carr, the presenter of our *Sport Spotlight* programme, would usually be at Ballacraine to provide an affable and accurate link between the ebullient Walkers.

In Motor Racing we were blessed with the expertise of Raymond Baxter, a Spitfire pilot during the war, and very much at home with all things mechanical. He was, and still is, a superb broadcaster, equally at home on radio or television, and was an admired presenter of *Tomorrow's World.* He is probably the only person who has taken part in the Monte Carlo Rally and broadcast about it as well. After that, Silverstone and Brands Hatch must have seemed like child's play. To the layman, and that includes me, one racing car looks very much like another. In expert hands the scene can come alive and the mysterious rites in the pits make sense. It has always seemed odd to me that, after so much careful attention from brilliant mechanics, so many things go wrong with the cars. Another puzzle to the layman is why the fastest car, presumably driven by the best driver, starts in front of all the others; not unlike the Derby favourite, ridden by the Champion Jockey, having a length start.

*British Grand Prix, Silverstone, July 1990.*

Despite Norman Tebbitt's advice to "get on your bike", we are not, by nature, a cycling nation; at least not in the same way as the French, for whom it is an obsessive pastime, or the Dutch, who have all that flat land to cycle on.

Accordingly, it was with some surprise, not to say alarm, that I heard from Benny Foster that the World Cycling Championships were to be held in Leicester from 6th to 16th August, 1970. Benny was the kingpin of cycling and had striven, with all his might, to bring the World Championships to Britain. All credit to him, and he fully deserved his OBE. As we already had, in that year, the Commonwealth Games in Edinburgh and the World Cup in Mexico, we in the BBC could frankly have done without them.

Cycling, in this country, receives minimal coverage, but the World Championships turned out to be a major operation in three locations in the Leicester area, attended by broadcasters from fifteen countries. This involved providing engineers, commentary positions, editing facilities, and many other technical and administrative requirements, for an event ninety-nine per cent of which would not be heard in Britain.

However, Benny did things in style. Ted Heath opened the Championships – arriving not by bike, but by car, to a salvo of blanks from the local Artillery regiment. Meanwhile, the broadcasters gabbled away in French, German, Dutch, Swedish, Spanish, Italian and a good many other languages. The sudden shortage of engineers for other programmes caused perplexity in many parts of the Corporation, which had never heard of the World Cycling Championships.


Sport has given me many new insights and experiences. Apart from Cricket and Rugby Union, in which I was an active player and participant at the microphone, my role, as Head of Outside Broadcasts, was mainly organisational. In this I invariably found help and support for what the BBC was trying to do. I was also able to sample the passions and enthusiasm of sportsmen and women for their own sport.

Sport is a national safety-valve of great importance. Long may it continue to be so.

The Queen's Birthday Parade is organised by the Brigade Major of the Household Division. It is not held on the Queen's Birthday and the Brigade Major is a Lieutenant Colonel. Nothing is quite what it seems!

This *Alice in Wonderland* world afflicted my first attempt at the radio commentary in 1961. "The Guards," I said, "are drawn up in a square rectangle, ready to be inspected by the Queen in their Bearskins".

An interesting picture, but not one to commend itself to the military choreographer who, each June, weaves his magic on Horse Guards Parade, surely the most dramatic stage in London.

Trooping the Colour, as it is generally known, dates back to the reign of Charles II, when the Colours of a Regiment were used as a rallying point and were regularly trooped in front of the soldiers, so they would recognise them. The present ceremony began in 1755 and, in 1805, the year of the Battle of Trafalgar, it was held for the first time on the Sovereign's birthday. Not inappropriately, Admiral Nelson casts his eye today, from the heights of his column, onto the shimmering symmetry of the Royal Procession as it turns off the Mall onto Horse Guards Parade.

Wars, strikes, illness and rain have, from time to time, caused the parade to be abandoned. Our present Queen has an enviable record, never having failed to take the

*Robert Hudson commentating on Trooping the Colour.*

salute, except in 1955, when a railway strike caused cancellation. Between 1961 and 1981, I, too, was ever present in my cramped commentary position, a type of dormer window high up in the Horse Guards Building.

Queen Victoria took the Salute only once. This was on her seventy-sixth birthday in 1895, when a parade was held in the Quadrangle of Windsor Castle. 'It was a very pretty sight,' she wrote in her diary, 'and the bands played extremely well'.

That was a royal understatement. Trooping the Colour by the Foot Guards, Household Cavalry and the Massed Bands is, beyond doubt, the most impressive military parade in the world. It is carried out each year, with apparently effortless efficiency, by the most 'laid back' body of men to be found anywhere. They are the best and don't have to be told so. But behind it all is meticulous attention to detail and repeated rehearsal.

It is a formidable broadcast for one commentator. It lasts one and a half hours and I needed all the help I could get. My preparation each year took two full weeks and included visits to the Regiment trooping its colour, to the Household Cavalry at Knightsbridge Barracks and to the band rehearsals at Chelsea Barracks. In the course of these, I would interview all the key figures in the parade and submit myself to the lavish hospitality of the Officers' Mess. A Guard's gin and tonic is quite unlike any other.

But let us leave the broadcaster and his problems for the time being. We will return to him later. What about the parade itself, and those who make it what it is – the annual object of frantic photography, for which tickets are like gold dust?

The three main ingredients are the marching of the Foot Guards, the riding of the Household Cavalry and the music of the Massed Bands. Each have their turn in the Spotlight: the Household Cavalry escort the Royal Procession from Buckingham Palace to Horse Guards Parade. The Queen then inspects the Parade. This is followed by the marching and counter-marching of the Massed Bands, a scintillating square of colour and sound. Then the No. 1 Guard, called the Escort, marches across to receive their Queen's Colour. This is then carried by the Ensign and trooped through the ranks of the other seven Guards. A Guard consists of three officers and seventy other ranks. The Foot Guards now march past in slow and quick time, followed by the Household Cavalry, at the walk and at the trot. Finally the Queen leads her Guards back to Buckingham Palace. Sounds simple, doesn't it? It isn't.

Let us start with the officer in command of the parade. He is a Guards officer, not a cavalryman, so he must learn to ride a horse. A docile and long-suffering animal is supplied, who won't mind his rider yelling, at the top of his voice, over one hundred words of command into his ears. On some occasions, many of the troops the officer is addressing are behind him and he has to project his voice to the Massed Bands and the Cavalry as well. No wonder one Commanding Officer took lessons at Covent Garden.

Some years ago, a small but heavy rifle was introduced, which was not long enough to reach the ground. The order 'Change Arms' has to be given at regular intervals to prevent the Guardsmen getting lop-sided.

The Colour itself is carried in a colour belt by a young Second Lieutenant, usually newly-commissioned from Sandhurst. It is a great honour and a great strain. The right elbow has to be kept up level with the chin for long periods; the young man will strengthen his arms with weight training and practise with a weight tied to the Colour, so that on the day it will seem lighter. He will never do it again in his whole life. His parents will be watching with pride as he lowers the Colour, in the march past, and the Queen salutes. I wish him luck.

Regimental Sergeant Majors, like policemen, seem to get younger. They also seem better educated and more even tempered than in my army days. Their recipe for success on parade is a good night's sleep, then some gentle physical training and a good breakfast. Fainting is a problem on a hot day, especially if your bearskin is too tight (it weighs nineteen ounces): solution – chew barley sugar, wriggle your toes and count the chimney pots on the Horse Guards Building.

What of the Guardsman himself? Contrary to popular conception, there is no lack of volunteers for this parade; to be in the No. 1 Guard is something to tell your grandchildren. His uniform is cleaned to perfection: no belt was ever whiter, no buttons have shone so brightly and he could use his boots as a shaving mirror. His bearskin cap, originally acquired from the French after their defeat at Waterloo, has been combed, washed and 'styled' like a human head of hair.

The horses of the Household Cavalry, most of whom come from Ireland, have been trained for their task in the Riding School, cossetted by their riders, and now wait phlegmatically in their stalls for the great day. They can be sure of a good meal of oats, bran and nuts when it is all over. They are shod with great care. One horse, dissatisfied with his footwear, is reputed to have walked into the farrier's shop and held his hoof up in disgust.

Only one in ten of their riders has ridden before joining the Army and yet in sixteen weeks of training, the last four in full dress, a new recruit could be riding past the Queen. It is a miraculous conversion from civilian life. But first he must get used to his helmet, to keeping his head still, and to being bolted fore and aft into his cuirasse, those gleaming breastplates of German silver, which look magnificent but feel like a sardine can. In addition, his jackboots and white gauntlets make him feel out of touch with his horse, with whom he naturally wishes to remain on the best of terms.

It will be a proud day, too, for the Squadron Corporal Major, who will carry the Sovereign's Standard and lower it in salute as he rides past the Queen. The Standard is crimson and gold with the Royal Coat of Arms and the Battle Honours emblazoned upon it. His wife and children will be watching. They will not forget.

You may be able to ride and to play an instrument but can you do both at once? That is the problem confronting the Mounted Bands of the Life Guards and the Blues and Royals, who combine to form one band about fifty strong. The two Drum Horses are in front, each with a silver drum two hundred years old and weighing half a hundredweight, on either flank. One of the horses had been spotted by the Queen, pulling a milk float in Edinburgh. Their riders control them by reins attached to their feet, while whirling the drumsticks above. Behind, stand six ranks of eight black horses, with a seventh rank of greys at the back for the clarinets. Most instruments require two hands, so the reins are looped over the arm. The musicians (never call them bandsmen) are spared the confines of breastplates; instead they wear magnificent Frock Coats of gold lace with black velvet caps. In front are the basses, euphoniums and tubas. In the rank behind, the slides of the trombones narrowly miss the horses' ears. On one occasion, despite the organised racket going on all round him, an old horse, carrying the Director of Music, went to sleep on parade.

It seems churlish to belittle the Mounted Bands, after all their efforts, but in comparison to the Massed Bands of the Grenadier, Coldstream, Scots, Irish and Welsh Guards, three hundred and eighty strong in nineteen ranks of twenty, and complete with Pipes and Drums, their output obviously sounds a little thin.

The music for the Queen's Birthday Parade reflects the Regiment whose Colour is being 'trooped'; perhaps an Irish flavour one year and a Welsh one the next. It is invariably marvellous and superbly played. The Major-General of the Household Division listens to it all before submitting it to the Queen, who gives final approval. After all, it is her 'Birthday'.

I came to know all the Directors of Music, over two decades, and always attended at least one band rehearsal, with my stop-watch and notebook. That way, and with their advice, I would calculate which parts of the music could safely be 'talked over' without losing the essential tune and rhythm. After my final broadcast in 1981, I was presented, by them, with a silver Cornet inscribed and made into a lampshade. On the way home with it by train, the eyes of the ticket collector at St Pancras station were popping out of his head. "Give us a tune, Guv," he said.


Let us return to my lofty window in the Horse Guards Building in 1981.

Sixteen pages of notes, pasted on cardboard, lie on an upturned box on the window ledge. I plan to give fifty-two separate pieces of commentary during the ninety-minute broadcast. Each will be preceded by a cue-light signal to our engineers in a small room behind. Instantly they lower the volume of sound behind my voice; a split-second operation.

It is 10.15. The spectators clutching their prized tickets have entered through the Horse Guards Arch. The eight thousand seats erected on three sides are filled with a mixture of morning dress, uniforms and summer frocks. The wise bring umbrellas as there is no cover. Stand in Whitehall and you will hear a babel of languages as they go in; tickets find their way to many foreign Embassies. It is predominantly a tourist attraction and the Mall and St James Park are also alive with visitors from many lands in casual holiday dress, each with a camera.

Gradually, the stage is filling as the Foot Guards come marching up from Chelsea Barracks. Some will have been driven to London by coach that morning from Caterham, Pirbright or Windsor.

The eight Guards make a vivid red inverted L-shape on the brown gravel of Horse Guards Parade. It is the turn of the Welsh Guards this year to troop their colour, now being held by the Colour Sergeant in front of No. 7 Guard. The Welsh supply two Guards, as do the Coldstream, Scots and Irish Guards. The Grenadier Guards are on duty elsewhere this year. Each Regiment marches on with its own band. All five bands mass in the left corner by 10 Downing Street. It looks as if the Prime Minister has taken the morning off; it would be hard to concentrate in the Cabinet room.

It is 10.45 and we are on the air. I pick up the 'lip' microphone which will be my companion for the next one and a half hours. In my headphones I hear the distant sounds of the Mounted Bands leading the Royal Procession from Buckingham Palace. In exactly fifteen minutes, as the clock on the roof strikes eleven, Her Majesty the Queen will be taking the salute in front of the Horse Guards Arch below me. Meanwhile, the Queen Mother arrives in an open carriage, followed, in the one behind, by Prince Andrew and Lady Diana Spencer, as she then was; to be married in eighteen days' time to the Prince of Wales. Her husband-to-be, as Colonel of the Welsh Guards, rides in the Royal Procession. The bearskin cap is an effective disguise, a cloak of anonymity; Prince Philip complained that its fringes in front of his eyes made him think it was raining. Sometimes it was. King George VI wore his, for practice, while gardening at Sandringham.

The Procession is making its stately way down the Mall, with Guardsmen lining the pavements, Union Jacks flying from the flagpoles and tens of thousands massed under the plane trees. First comes the Brigade Major, then the Mounted Bands with the lumbering Drum Horses, in effect setting the pace. Then the Life Guards, the epitome of martial splendour, breastplates glistening like mirrors, backs as straight as their drawn swords. Then the Queen, on her faithful horse Burmese, followed by the Blues and Royals: in theory she is 'protected', yet displayed. Too much so, perhaps, as a blank cartridge pistol is fired in her direction. It is out of my sight, but as the Procession turns onto Horse Guards Parade, it is clear that some horses are out of position. Burmese, whom the Queen rode for eighteen years, is temporarily startled, but at once brought under control by experienced horsemanship. The Queen faces her

*A blank cartridge pistol is fired at the Queen at Trooping the Colour, 1981.*

Guards. The Bands play the National Anthem. The clock is striking eleven.

The Queen, the only woman among 1,134 men, contrives to look both regal and graceful as she inspects the parade. She rides side-saddle, followed by the Royal Princes, her red uniform offset by a dark blue habit; in her black tricorn hat is the green and white plume of the Welsh Guards. Burmese seems to know the way without being told. Sadly, Burmese is now dead and the Queen drives in a carriage.

I look for gaps in the music. The Inspection is accompanied by lilting Welsh tunes; then there is silence for two and a half minutes as the Queen's Procession rides back to the Saluting Base. I use this time to signpost ahead – to put the listener in the picture.

The Massed Bands now take the stage, marching and counter-marching in slow and quick time. Trombones, cornets, euphoniums and the 55 lb tuba (try carrying that for three hours) meet the horns, saxophones, clarinets and piccolos coming the other way; not to mention the drums and pipes. It is riveting to ear and eye.

All this has been set in motion by the one order 'Troop' from Colonel Gaussen. I am glad to note he is in good voice; important to the BBC – we need to hear him.

A single drummer beats *Drummer's Call*, the signal for the Escort to march out and receive the Queen's Colour. The Lieutenant of the Escort takes command. In 1748, when a special Guard was mounted for the first time on the King's birthday, it was commanded by a subaltern. So the same thing happens today.

I have a valuable one minute and eighteen seconds before *The British Grenadiers* sends them on their way across Horse Guards Parade; by judicious planning, they narrowly miss the Massed Bands who execute a remarkable 'Spin Wheel' to manoeuvre out of their way. In this they pivot on their centre and end up facing in the other direction, leaving Horse Guards Parade clear for the Escort. It is not in the Drill Book but seems to be passed down from father to son.

The Regimental Sergeant Major draws his sword and delivers the Colour to the young Ensign whose heavy ordeal begins.

Having secured the Colour, the No. 1 Guard becomes Escort 'to', not 'for', the Colour. I pause to allow the revised words of command to be heard. The Colour is trooped through the ranks. The music captures the solemn mood of the moment. However, it goes on for quite a long time, so I recall the heroic deeds of the Welsh Guards, not least their dramatic dash to Brussels in the last War. All the time, I try to build up the scene and describe the action in relation to my own position. Wherever I can, I explain the symbolic meaning of each movement and look ahead to the next, but also let all the best of the music be heard. It is a fascinating challenge. By my twenty-first attempt I had become quite good at it.

Now for the march-past, first in slow, then in quick, time.

Horse Guards Parade is not as flat as it looks. There are drains and undulations. Marching on it is not easy. The sixteen ranks revolve like the spokes of a wheel at each corner; then come marching past the Queen like so

Above: *Trooping the Colour, 1983.*

many red pencils. The Ensign lowers the Colour perfectly. How proud he must feel, as the Queen salutes.

Slick work by the Massed Bands, not least in changing their music, produces each Regimental Slow March at exactly the right moment: *Men of Harlech* for the Welsh. Then the Quick March Past; so much more difficult. If the ranks become a bit wavy, correct them slowly; then eyes right to the Queen.

Finally the Household Cavalry rank past at the walk and at the trot: the Rolls Royces of the cavalry world. First the Life Guards, with white plumes in their helmets and white sheepskins on their horses; then the Blues and Royals with red plumes and black sheepskins. In all, eight ranks of twelve horses; my cue light is red hot, the pace frantic, as *The Keel Row* echoes round Horse Guards Parade.

Now the stage is re-set, with the component parts back where they started. Colonel Gaussen rides up to the Queen to report that, "Your Majesty's Guards are ready to march off, Ma'am". We strain our supersensitive microphones to catch what he says. I had asked him to speak up at this point, but one can't shout at one's Queen. He finds a happy compromise. We hear him perfectly.

Then, with the Queen at their head, the Guards swing away back to Buckingham Palace.

These fighting men of the modern mechanised Army have turned temporarily to a Ceremonial role. Tomorrow, some will be on Guard Duty at Buckingham Palace and St James's Palace, but most will be back training as infantry or in tanks or armoured cars. But today they have brought to life centuries of tradition with a flair, precision and style, unique to the Household Division.

They have lived up to that famous motto:

*NULLI SECUNDUS* – Second to None.

# CHAPTER 16
# Eventful Days

"He's sitting up in bed, drinking a cup of coffee," said the voice in my headphones. It was the lunch interval at Bramall Lane, Sheffield, in 1963. I was broadcasting the 'Roses' match – the biennial, and rather grim, encounter between Yorkshire and Lancashire on the cricket field. I was also 'on call' to describe the funeral of Pope John in Rome. His medical condition was thus of some personal interest and concern. As a Staff Commentator, I had long ceased to be surprised by anything.

The Pope survived until close of play, but the next day found me in the Crypt of St Peter's, Rome, discussing plans for his funeral, fortified, rather incongruously, by beer and sandwiches supplied by Vatican Radio.

I am not a Roman Catholic, but could not fail to admire the restrained splendour of the funeral and the speed with which it was organised; so rapidly indeed that, two days later, I was able to be at my usual window in the Horse Guards building in Whitehall for Trooping the Colour. This was just as well, as I had spent most of the previous fortnight preparing for it.

A week as varied as Heinz Soup ended with the installation, in Brighton, of Viscount Monckton as Chancellor of the University of Sussex and a live broadcast, from Victoria Station, of the arrival of the President of India on a State Visit. Life certainly was not dull.

Relieved of all administrative and production duties, a staff commentator was expected, within reason, to broadcast anything, anywhere, at any time, either on radio or TV. My colleagues were Brian Johnston and Raymond Baxter, but it was rare for all of us to be in the office together. Our salaries were the only fixed elements of our lives. There were no set hours and certainly no overtime. You did whatever was required. It was a wonderful job. It had taken me seven years on the staff to achieve this dream occupation via production, microphone and administrative duties in the North Region. My first assignment there in 1954 had also very nearly been my last.

Gilbert Harding, a man of uncertain temper and idiosyncratic outlook, was to conduct a live radio interview with, if I recall correctly, Beatrice Lillie, during the interval at a theatre in Manchester. His verbal explosions on *Twenty Questions* had already achieved notoriety. My job was to see that all went well, soberly and to time. This was easier said than done. On the one hand I had to ensure that the performance started promptly so that the interval would coincide with our slot in the Light Programme. On the other, I had, somehow, to stem the flow of whisky down Gilbert's throat. Failing in this latter objective, I acquired a plate of sandwiches from the theatre bar and, by determined force-feeding, managed to counteract the effect on Gilbert of alarming quantities of Scotch. Later that same year, Gilbert switched on the Blackpool Illuminations: the ultimate accolade for a celebrity. I was deputed to describe this visual extravaganza on the radio; not, I might add, an easy thing to do. Television had not yet reached Blackpool.

The fifties were daring years for radio; a last fling perhaps before the pre-eminence of TV. With Denis Mitchell, a gifted features producer, I organised several large-scale broadcasts of Northern cities. By combining carefully-edited recordings and live outside broadcasts, linked by a professional narrator, we aimed to create pictures, in the mind, of Liverpool, Sheffield and Newcastle.

For our programme on Hull, we placed Wynford Vaughan Thomas in a mobile transmitting van and gave him a police escort. Wynford, who was game for anything, then toured the City, dropping in at six varied but carefully-prepared 'OB' locations, including the Mayor's Parlour and a rather seedy Music Hall, to get the flavour of Hull. While Wynford was on the move, we played pre-recorded material from the studio. It was a tour de force for Wynford, but nearly gave me heart failure. For a *Nightout* in the Isle of Man, Philip Robinson, the narrator, was in a horse tram moving along the seafront at Douglas, linking theatres, dance halls and holiday camps, to illustrate the range of entertainment on the island. Everything was done live with split-second timing and, of course, much depended on our wonderful engineers. Nothing like that happens today. It is safer and cheaper to pre-record; but how much duller.

In 1960 I found myself in Lagos for the birth of the independent nation of

Nigeria. Princess Alexandra represented the Queen, who does not personally give away the Empire. My commentary position, a rather rickety scaffolding on Lagos Racecourse, seemed in danger of collapse as the Union Jack came down at midnight and the green and black flag of Nigeria took its place. My cheerful colleagues of the Nigerian Broadcasting Corporation produced bottled beer in large quantities and a good, if somewhat dangerous, time was had by all.

*Princess Alexandra declares the Independence of Nigeria, Lagos, 1960.*

I could detect little animosity towards Britain; in fact, quite the reverse. Fifty years before, there had been no railways, few roads, no motor cars and no aeroplanes. Now, wide roads led to schools, churches, shops, hospitals and all the adjuncts of modern civilisation. Sadly, these tangible assets do not guarantee a stable future. Princess Alexandra, elegant in a full-length dress, white gloves and tiara, handed over the Independence Constitution in a ceremony the next day, which I also broadcast. But difficult times for the new Nigeria were to lie ahead.

Independence ceremonies, in other parts of Africa, followed an almost identical pattern. A quick check, to confirm that the same British officer was in charge, and my notes, carefully prepared in Nigeria, stood me in good stead in Kenya and Tanzania. The difficulties were of a more unusual type. A colossal traffic jam to the stadium outside Nairobi meant that I only just kept my date with the BBC. In Dar-es-Salaam a church service to celebrate Independence was to be attended by Prince Philip. Unfortunately, he was seventeen minutes late; my vigil at the church door for a 'brief scene-set' became an unexpected nightmare. Luckily, the service took place in the Church of St Alban and, living in St Albans, I was able to compare it – in some detail – with St Albans Abbey. Nevertheless, the eventual arrival of His Royal Highness was more than usually welcome.

For twenty-one years it was my pleasure to introduce the programme of *Christmas Bells* which, in those days (1965 to 1985), immediately preceded the Queen's Christmas Message on the Home Service, later to be Radio 4. I came to know and admire the ringers and their ways. England is the home of 'change ringing'. Some people imagine that the ringers change places. This is not so. They stay put and so do the bells. It is the order in which they are rung which changes and very complex that can be.

Fabian Stedman, a Cambridge printer, has been the cause of much mental and physical exercise by countless ringers, young and old. In about 1668, he became tired of ringing in a regular sequence and started to experiment, with startling and complicated results. Age does not matter and ringers from twelve to ninety-two have figured in our broadcasts. They need to be fit, have a good sense of rhythm and a head for heights and mental arithmetic. Ringing runs in families and romance flourishes. At Maidstone in 1985 Tom Cullingworth, the Tower Captain, had been ringing for sixty years and his wife, Lily, for fifty-six. Needless to say, they met in a bell tower.

We would include seven churches, from all parts of the United Kingdom, in our twenty-five minute programme; from the North, Midlands, south and south-west of England and also from Scotland, Wales and Northern Ireland. In my narration, I tried to explain the mechanics of ringing and to talk to the people who did it. Before you can tackle any of Fabian Stedman's fiendish permutations, you must master the art of controlling a bell – by no means a simple matter. Then study at home, with pen and paper, tracing the 'course' of your own bell in a particular 'method', then try to put it into practice with the other ringers, entirely from memory. The men would be in shirt sleeves; the ladies favour cardigans and sensible shoes. A schoolboy would be on the 'treble', the lightest bell, and a burly blacksmith-type man on the heavy tenor. Common to them all was an air of fierce concentration. A 'peal' is 5,040 'changes' and takes about three hours to ring. It has to be done perfectly to count in the records. Popularity suffers if you make a mistake on the 5,035th change.

I must have climbed at least eighty towers in the course of presenting this programme, as I tried to visit as many as possible. I suffered both claustrophobia on the narrow winding stone staircases and sometimes dizziness at the steep drop down to the Nave. Dr Runcie, as Archbishop of Canterbury, and David Sheppard, Bishop of Liverpool and a former England cricket captain, have both given me interviews on the programme; the recording of the latter was delayed a little while we discussed the Bishop's innings at the Oval against Pakistan in 1962, which I had described on *Test Match Special*. In 1985, we began our programme at Romsey Abbey in Hampshire where, on a plain black stone, are these words:

Admiral of the Fleet, Earl Mountbatten of Burma 1900 to 1979
In Honour Bound

My mind went back to a rehearsal of Trooping the Colour, a few weeks before he died, when Lord Mountbatten as Colonel of the Life Guards had taken the salute. Also to a jungle clearing, nearly thirty-five years earlier, when as Commander-in-Chief South East Asia he stood on a box and, in uplifting style, addressed the officers and men of my artillery battery. What war failed to do was achieved by the IRA.

His funeral in Westminster Abbey, on 5th September 1979, was a good example of an old-fashioned outside broadcast. The four commentators had all served in the last war. We handed the commentary on to each other without recourse to any recorded gimmicks. We knew our jobs and we sensed the occasion. Alun Williams, in the Mall, and myself, in the Abbey, had both served in the Far East; Raymond Baxter spoke from Whitehall and Godfrey Talbot was on the roof of the Henry VII Chapel. It was, I believe, a professional and very moving broadcast. It was not achieved without effort.

The murderous death of Lord Mountbatten left little time to prepare. The ceremonial document detailing the impressive funeral procession, in which his horse Dolly took part, with his riding boots reversed in the stirrups, and the Order of Service itself were only available at the last moment. As a consequence I worked all night on my notes in my hotel room near the Abbey. My view next day was from high up in the triforium as the coffin was carried in by naval ratings. The Queen and the Royal Family were in the Sanctuary. Prince Charles read the lesson. It was a memorable farewell to a remarkable man.

It so happens that I am the only person, alive or dead, who has 'enthroned' three Archbishops of Canterbury. My appearances in the organ loft of Canterbury Cathedral spanned nineteen years from 1961 (Dr Ramsey) to 1980 (Dr Runcie), with Dr Coggan coming between them in 1975. *Guinness Book of Records* please note!

Dr Ramsey, looking much older than he was, brought his dog to the rehearsal, which seemed a human touch. Dr Coggan was kind enough to write to me, after his Enthronement, to thank me for my commentary on it, to which he had apparently listened later.

Dr Runcie, at one time my own bishop of St Albans, was helpful in many ways, not least in giving a protracted kiss to the Canterbury Gospels, in order to allow me sufficient time to describe what he was doing. He also met Tom Fleming, who was giving the TV commentary, and myself, before the Enthronement, to clarify various points and explain their symbolic significance. It is an intricate ceremony, to which I had to devote much thought in order to convey a clear picture to listeners without cutting across the service. We would normally produce an edited version, for the World Service, in the early evening. This would be transmitted from the small self-operated Canterbury studio. In 1980, that admirable broadcaster Gerald Priestland, who had been giving a news piece from the studio, unfortunately went home with the key. An awkward gap loomed in the World Service schedules. The situation was saved by an enterprising engineer, who made a hectic dash by car to BBC Radio Medway to get another key, while I was still writing the linking script. It was a near thing, but the world heard, with two minutes to spare, that we had a new Archbishop of Canterbury.

BBC planners do not welcome an event of this sort, which cannot be accurately foreseen, and which tends to clash with established programmes. In

1975, as Head of Outside Broadcasts, I was having difficulty in obtaining the one and a half hours needed for a live broadcast. "Can't we record it and put out extracts later?" was the query. My reply was ready: "We enthroned the Pope 'live' and in full". There is no answer to that.

The Pope paid a visit to Canterbury Cathedral on a memorable occasion in 1982. At the rehearsal, we were told that the Archbishop and the Pope would walk up the Nave together, turn inwards for prayers, and walk together again to the High Altar. I asked one of the junior clergy what he thought would happen if one of them got a short lead on the other. "I think," he said, "it will be end of Christianity as we know it".

Live broadcasts of banquets are not for the faint-hearted. Much depends on the caterers, quite brilliant at the Guildhall in London for the Lord Mayor's Banquet, but less reliable elsewhere. On a State Visit overseas King George VI had to make his broadcast speech in the middle of the meal. My own initiation was at Manchester Town Hall in 1954. Sensing trouble, I held a Council of War with the Master of Ceremonies, the head caterer, the Lord Mayor of Manchester and Lord Woolton, who was to propose a toast to the Cotton Trade. I explained the cue light system and the absolute necessity of serving the meal on time. My scene-set would be two minutes, delivered from behind a screen in a corner of the room, and then, at 8.32 exactly, they could expect the green light. The MC must then leap at once into action, regardless of the progress of the meal. In the event, it was a dead heat with the coffee but my team did not let me down and I survived to fight another day.

At the Guildhall, the live radio broadcast began at 9.15 and usually found me, in white tie and tails, sharing a gallery with residual members of the Lord Mayor's family. Ring and Brymer, the caterers, by impeccable organisation, would contrive to serve the eight hundred diners with turtle soup, roast beef and much more besides, in plenty of time. However, the speeches could not begin until after the 'scene-set' which took about two minutes. Churchill would often chafe at this delay. The speeches by the Lord Mayor and the Prime Minister would be announced with a fanfare by a trumpeter of the Household Cavalry – on one occasion missing, due to a call of nature. Then the Toastmaster would have his moment of glory. These gentlemen tend to be rather full of their own importance. "You'll have to speak up, your Grace," was the advice of one of them to an Archbishop, as he rose to speak, "the agnostics are terrible".

In 1967, in addition to broadcasting cricket every weekday for two months, a classic example of too much of a good thing, I found myself in another varied selection of places. For example, I welcomed back Sir Francis Chichester after his circumnavigation of the globe, from behind a pillar on the balcony of the Mansion House. The little man, with his jaunty yachting cap, came up the steps to speak to the thousands who jammed the road outside. He had been knighted by the Queen at Greenwich, with Raymond Baxter in attendance, and now we broke live into the Home Service, just before a lunch given in his honour by the Lord Mayor.

On Trafalgar Day, I kept a regular date with Admiral Nelson for a pleasant and nostalgic broadcast from Trafalgar Square. Nowadays, the great deeds of 1805 go largely unremembered. In April of 1967, I went with Ian Trethowan, later to become Director General of the BBC, to cover the funeral of Dr Adenauer in Cologne. I recall the American President, Lyndon Johnson, and President de Gaulle, passing close to my commentary position at the bottom of the Cathedral steps as the coffin was carried out. Luckily the radio broadcast ended at that point, but Ian Trethowan, on television, was in some difficulty as timings of the journey up the Rhine went seriously awry.

As Head of Outside Broadcasts, I found, as a general rule, that it was unwise both to take responsibility for the worldwide coverage of a major event and also to take part in the broadcast. Many a newspaper editor must yearn to be out in the field, but he is probably better advised to stay at his desk. For the marriage of Princess Anne to Captain Mark Phillips in 1973 I broke my own rule and stationed myself outside Westminster Abbey. There was naturally great interest from overseas and my next door neighbour in the line of commentary boxes was from the United States. His knowledge of British Ceremonial appeared to be sketchy. The Yeomen of the Guard are often referred to as 'Beefeaters', although this expression strictly applies to the Yeomen Warders of

Left: *Robert Hudson commentating on the Silver Jubilee.* Right: *John Haslam, later Deputy Press Secretary to the Queen.*

the Tower of London. My American colleague had his own version. "The aisle of the church," he told his 'coast to coast' audience, "is to be lined by Beefburgers".

The Royal Family always sit on the right, even when a daughter is getting married. I went into the Abbey after the service. On each Royal Chair lay the Order of Service. On the left, where the Phillips family had been sitting, every chair was empty. This sort of thing didn't often happen to them.

The celebration of Silver Jubilees only began in the twentieth century. King George V set the precedent in 1935. The broadcast of it was the last big occasion of the radio-only era. Queen Elizabeth I had ignored her twenty-fifth anniversary in 1583 and Queen Victoria was still in mourning for Prince Albert in 1862. The Silver Jubilee of Queen Elizabeth II was, in reality, three months of

*Morning rehearsal of Queen Elizabeth II's Silver Jubilee procession.*

national celebration from early May to the end of July, with the service in St Paul's on June 7th as the focal point. I described this, from high up in the West Gallery and made a little bit of history by so doing: in 1935 the commentator had to stay outside.

My knowledge of the Cathedral came in handy. Few knew, but I did, that halfway along the North side of the triforium was a flushing lavatory. This surprising, but priceless, information, not unlike discovering an oasis in the desert, was to make me the hero of the hour among the cable layers, photographers and trumpeters, whose duties made them temporary tenants of the triforium. The alternative was to follow the 500 feet of cable leading from my microphone down the spiral staircase, along the full length of the Nave, and then down to the Crypt, where our engineers were more handily placed.

*Silver Jubilee of Queen Elizabeth II, 1977. The Royal Family on the balcony of Buckingham Palace.*

The Silver Jubilee was a Royal, not a State, occasion. As such, it was masterminded by the Lord Chamberlain, not the Earl Marshal. The service was a happy one. The Dean was a friendly New Zealander, Dr Martin Sullivan. I asked him what he would say to the Queen when she arrived. "I shall say," he replied, "it is a great honour, your Majesty, to welcome you to St Paul's Cathedral on your Silver Jubilee," which seemed fair enough. One couldn't argue with it.

A Royal Family conference had clearly taken place to avoid colour clashes. The Queen was in pink, the Queen Mother in yellow, Princess Anne in blue and the Duchess of Kent in green. Prince Charles had ridden at the rear wheel of the Gold State Coach, as Colonel of the Welsh Guards, but anonymous in his black bearskin cap. He found kneeling with a sword too much of a problem and gave it up as a bad job.

The masterstroke was the 'walkabout', from St Paul's to the Guildhall, which made the Queen late for the Civic Luncheon, but which plainly delighted Her Majesty and everyone else as well. Brian Johnston, following with a portable transmitter, asked Prince Philip to say a few words on the air: "I'd like to," he said, "but I can't hear myself think". Meanwhile, it was reported from Blackheath that exactly five people attended an anti-monarchist rally.

The four of us, Rex Alston, Brian Johnston, Raymond Baxter and myself, who were, at various times, staff commentators for the BBC, realised, I am sure, how lucky we were to lead a life of exceptional variety and interest, but within the security of a staff salary. In return, we did our utmost to do a good job on each and every occasion. With me, the key factor was time to prepare. Given this, I had few worries. Preparation breeds confidence and that is essential for success at the microphone. At times, though, there barely seemed enough hours in the day.

# CHAPTER 17
# Head of Outside Broadcasts

"Don't touch it with a bargepole": the reaction of a respected senior colleague in the BBC. I had been invited to leave my job as a Staff Commentator and instead become Head of the Radio Outside Broadcasts Department. To his way of thinking, this looked like a voluntary transfer from heaven to hell. He had a point.

'OBs' had a notable past, but an uncertain future. The department had been a star in the BBC firmament in the golden age of the wireless. It had spawned famous names like Raymond Glendenning, Wynford Vaughan Thomas, Stewart Macpherson, Rex Alston, Max Robertson, Brian Johnston, Raymond Baxter and not least the unpredictable Gilbert Harding. For twenty-one years from 1946 – 1967 Wilfred Pickles had introduced *Have a Go* as a live OB. It was masterminded by Stephen Williams, the creator of Radio Luxembourg. This galaxy of stars was kept in some sort of order by Frank ('Spike') Anderson, the Administrative Officer and a long-time friend of mine. But now it was 1969; television ruled the roost and the view was that the broadcasting of sport and events on the radio had had its day. Everyone would watch television.

I doubted this. If you watch television, you can't easily do anything else; radio, on the other hand, can be your companion in the kitchen and the car, at your bedside, on the beach or in the garden. For the cricket scores, it can hide in your school or office desk. To be sure we were in the television age; but also in the age of the transistor and the car radio.

A document was produced called *Broadcasting in the Seventies*, which did nothing to cheer me up. Sport was not mentioned, nor was the OB Department. I seemed to be in charge of a ghost. To make matters worse, many of the star performers had left to go freelance and of those who remained some were of long and worthy service and soon to retire.

Internal politics are endemic to any large organisation, so I will be brief. Suffice it to say that departmentalism was, and presumably still is, a major

*Gilbert Harding*

bugbear in the BBC. Many programmes are on the borderline and two departments may lay claim to them.

Sport was such a case.

Two floors up from OBs in Broadcasting House, there lurked the Sports News Department, staffed by bright young men (the bright young women came later), under the leadership of Angus Mackay, a crusty, but brilliantly innovative, Scot. He had launched *Sports Report* in 1948 and had forged a highly effective partnership with its presenter Eamonn Andrews. It was the jewel in their crown.

The function of Sports News was to report sport, in journalistic style, after the event. In OBs, we described it as it happened. We also controlled the technical facilities and negotiated contracts with the sporting authorities. Over the years, bad blood had developed between the two departments, which should never have been created separately in the first place. For example, two people, both involved in broadcasting the same sport, did not speak to each other for ten years. Messages were passed through a third party: incredible but true.

The obvious solution was an amalgamation, a less emotive word than 'takeover'. However, Sports News formed part of the News Division and one didn't remove bits of that empire with impunity.

Luckily, the new Managing Director of Radio was to be Ian Trethowan, later to become Director General of the BBC. He happened to be a sports enthusiast and had no intention of allowing Radio to take a back seat on national occasions, sporting or otherwise. The future began to look rosier. I took my seat at Heads of Department meetings, alongside my colleagues from Drama, Light Entertainment, Religion, Talks and Features, with renewed hope that OBs would not only continue to exist, but might actually increase and improve its output.

Frank Gillard had appointed me Head of Radio Outside Broadcasts in 1969, but was to retire at the end of the year, so the future lay with Ian Trethowan. With his approval, I signed long-term contracts, exclusive to BBC Radio, with the Football, Cricket, Rugby Union, Racing, Athletics and Golf authorities. In general, I steered clear of making a joint approach with BBC Television, in case Radio should lose a contract in the process. Lawn Tennis was an exception and Radio was included in Peter Dimmock's Television agreement with the Wimbledon authorities. I also laid plans for amalgamating the two warring departments. It was a bizarre situation, as our rivals upstairs were apparently hatching similar plans in the reverse direction!

However OBs, with the contracts safely signed and our link with the engineers intact, clearly held most of the aces.

I felt that Sports News would be ill-advised to bite the hand that fed it. Finally Desmond Taylor, the Editor of News and Current Affairs, in a statesmanlike gesture, accepted this view and it was agreed that an amalgamation should take place, under my leadership, and within the Radio, not the News, Directorate. It was finally achieved on 1st August 1973, after the retirement of Angus Mackay.

My experience as Head of Administration in the North and as a Personnel Manager in industry, before joining the BBC, stood me in good stead. Most problems are human in origin. How easy life would be without people! Money, for example, can't answer back; add it up, spend it or save it. Problems of planning and organisation may be difficult but they don't have fits of the sulks. Human problems are the most intractable and difficult to solve. I had enough to last a lifetime.

The BBC has a strong sense of vertical organisation. It expects its staff to progress, in an orderly manner, up either the Production, Administration or Engineering ladder. My own zig-zagging performance between Production, Administration and Microphone work was a source of some perplexity. However, it left me in a strong position. The activities of shadowy but powerful departments, such as Staff Administration, Grading, Appointments and Accounts, were familiar to me from my experience as an Administrator. Wearing my programme hat, I had a clear idea of the quantity and quality of output which the OB department should seek to achieve. In short, it would be difficult to pull the wool over my eyes.

My happy life at the microphone was largely over, although I continued to broadcast some of the big events myself in the years ahead. The BBC, at that time, had a comically maternal urge to protect the creative performer from the hideous realities of administration and management. Tiresome problems of staff, accommodation and money might staunch the flow of brilliant thoughts which they would otherwise, no doubt, be bringing to the air-waves and the screen.

Now, no longer divorced in this way from reality, I found myself with a staff of fifty-five, a budget of half a million pounds (a lot in those days) and the additional task of fusing two feuding groups into a homogeneous whole.

At a conservative estimate, my new job was ten times more difficult than my old one. The contrast was laughable. In recognition of this, my salary was increased by one hundred pounds a year!

In 1969, the Outside Broadcasts Department had a hand, even if only a technical one, in virtually everything that was broadcast outside the studio. Frank Howard, the senior engineer, was linked to me on the programme side by means of a jointly manned Booking Office.

Sometimes, when our technical resources became unduly stretched, he would call on me to exercise the wisdom of Solomon. Were we to give the United States yet more facilities at Wimbledon or broadcast Evensong from Canterbury Cathedral? We couldn't do both. A straight choice between Mammon and God.

Those of us directly involved with programme output had a close working relationship with our Outside Broadcast engineers. We not only respected people like Frank Howard, Johnny Ford, Leo Feord, Dick Elsden, Phil Older and many others for their technical skill, but also valued their friendship and support.

Over the years, the department had acquired a number of prestigious programmes. *Down Your Way* and *Pick of the Week* were produced by Phyllis Robinson and Richard Burwood. Judging by the pins in the map on the office wall, *Down Your Way* had nowhere left to go: eventually taken off, it had to be brought back by popular demand. Its presenters had been Richard Dimbleby, Franklin Engelmann and Brian Johnston; its tone friendly and non-controversial.

We were responsible for the delightful *Countryside* programmes and for the fast-moving quiz broadcasts *Treble Chance* and *Sporting Chance*, masterminded by Michael Tuke-Hastings, who also took *Forces' Chance* to various outposts of the Empire to entertain the troops.

Finally, the Motoring Unit, presided over by Jim Pestridge and an able team of ex-police officers, did a brisk trade in accidents, fog warnings, traffic jams and burst water mains; 'load shedding', of remarkable diversity, was also a popular feature. *Motoring and the Motorist* took a weekly look at motoring problems.

So we had a mixed bag of output and a finger in most pies.

The eventual amalgamation with Sports News produced a dramatic injection of youth and talent. The new Radio Sports Unit was controlled by Cliff Morgan, one of the few people who seems to have solved the problem of being in two places at once. During his twenty-nine appearances on the rugby field for Wales, wing-forwards chased his shadow without much success. As Sports Editor his gregarious enthusiasm and wide contacts in the world of sport were invaluable. He seemed omnipresent. Cliff went on to succeed me and then became Head of Television Outside Broadcasts.

The Assistant Sports Editor was Bob Burrows, later to leave the BBC to become a leading light in ITV Sport and win for them the coverage of the Rugby Union World Cup. He was a brilliant Editor.

Our Saturday Sports programme had found a new home on Radio 2 and was presented by Desmond Lynam, now the best and most experienced of television sports presenters, and by Peter Jones, a most able broadcaster, who sadly died at the microphone while giving a commentary on the Boat Race. Several others in the Sports Unit went on to fame and, I trust, fortune in television or journalism; not least Christopher Martin-Jenkins, destined to follow E.W. Swanton as the Cricket Correspondent of *The Daily Telegraph,* and John Motson, later to be television's leading football commentator. The only casualty of the amalgamation was Jacob de Vries, who had been an excellent Senior Sports Producer but decided not to accept the post he was offered.

In fast-moving sports broadcasting, there tends to be a conflict of views between the producer, at the hub of affairs in the bowels of Broadcasting House, and the commentators on the rim of the wheel, with eyes only for their own event. The man in the studio, in possession of all the facts, decides where to go next as he darts about the country in search of the most compelling broadcasting and the latest news. His judgement, not unnaturally, is often questioned by those at the sharp end, who find their splendid commentary curtailed in favour of some footling occurrence elsewhere.

Education in the different roles was needed. The 'inside' man had to learn to appreciate the problems of a commentator with the crowd yelling all round him. Those 'outside' had to understand the pressures and responsibilities of the studio-based producer.

Soon, understanding was developed and the Sports Unit settled down to the professional performance we now take for granted. Its talented staff could spread their wings.

While negotiating the details of this amalgamation, I was also heavily involved in planning the coverage of major events, among them the Investiture of the Prince of Wales in 1969, the Commonwealth Games and the World Cup in 1970, and the Olympic Games in Munich in 1972.

The public do not appreciate what a big part the BBC is called upon to play in helping foreign and Commonwealth broadcasters. For example, the marriage of Princess Anne and Captain Mark Phillips in 1973 was broadcast in twenty-four languages. A number of these broadcasts were made by the BBC's own External Services, but we also provided technical facilities, commentary positions, engineers and programme information for commentators from Australia, Austria, Belgium, France, Germany, Holland, Luxembourg, Monaco, New Zealand, Sri Lanka and the United States (ABC and CBS). Our own domestic and World Service coverage was but the tip of the iceberg.

As host country we bear a heavy load, particularly on major Royal Occasions, which seem to act as a magnet to the rest of the world. But our responsibilities to the Commonwealth extended, in my time at least, to events abroad as well.

For example, at the Olympic Games in Munich in 1972, I led a radio team of fifty-six, including no less than eighteen engineers: enough to service the needs of Australia, New Zealand, West Indies, Kenya, India, Malawi, Nigeria, Bahamas and Cyprus. We had seven studios, all working flat out, and connected as required to Outside Broadcasts points throughout the Olympic complex and to the relevant mother country. Our own domestic output, and that of the World Service, was channelled down one permanent line to a special control room on the second floor of Broadcasting House. Here a producer was always on duty to switch the material, pouring down the line from Munich, in the right direction: perhaps to the *Today* studio, for an interview, or to Bush House for a thirty-minute World Service programme. Then to the News Studio or to the main Sports Network for live commentary; finally to a recording studio for a succession of 'packaged' items aimed at specific local radio stations. That line was buzzing all day and for much of the night as well.

The Germans were efficient but inflexible. Peter Baxter, in charge of the complicated scheduling arrangements, was a calming influence on Indian Hockey commentators and German bureaucrats alike. I enjoyed those high-powered occasions, not least the organisation and planning. To meet the needs not only of the BBC, but, seemingly, of much of the rest of the world as well, was a source of great satisfaction.

I was Head of Outside Broadcasts for six years to the day.

In 1975, I left the BBC to help my wife with her Antiques business, to continue broadcasting as a freelance, and to start a new career as a lecturer. They had been years of rich variety, some worry and much happiness. Far from being out of business, the OB department had, in 1975, broadcast more hours of sport, events and other programmes than ever before. A week's output in my time might have looked like this:

| | | |
|---|---|---|
| LORDS: | England v Australia | *Pick of the Week* |
| WIMBLEDON: | Lawn Tennis Championships | *Down Your Way* |
| AUCKLAND: | New Zealand v British Lions | *Motoring and the Motorist* |
| WINDSOR: | Garter Ceremony | *Sport on Two* |
| WEMBLEY: | Boxing | *The Countryside in Summer* |
| ROME: | Enthronement of the Pope | *Treble Chance* |

It seemed to me that despite television, Radio Outside Broadcasts were still in business! Now the Department, and the BBC as a whole, face new and difficult problems in the nineties. Their solution will not be easy. I wish them well.

# CHAPTER 18
# Saint George's Chapel

"It is our pleasure that His Royal Highness, the Prince of Wales, and the Knight Companions, newly invested, be Installed."

Her Majesty the Queen was standing at the entrance to the mellow magnificence of the Choir of St George's Chapel, Windsor. Facing her on the black and white marble floor, between choirstalls of English oak, stood her son, aged nineteen, together with Lord de L'Isle, V.C. and Lord Amory. It was 17th June 1968 and my first experience of broadcasting from one of the most beautiful places in Britain. Prince Charles was to be installed as a Knight of the Garter.

The procession had wound its way down the road from the Castle. It was led by the Military Knights of Windsor, Soldiers of Honour, who live within the grey stone walls. They wore scarlet swallowtail coats and cocked hats. On one occasion, setting too slow a pace, the procession had been late. The following year, encouraged, apparently by the Queen, to walk a bit faster, they reached the West Door two minutes early, causing some difficulty for the commentator. Being early is, if anything, worse than being late.

The route is downhill, but the well-being not only of the Military Knights, but also of elderly Knights of the Garter, in their heavy blue mantles and black velvet hats, has to be taken into account; particularly on a hot June day after a substantial lunch.

*Robert Hudson commentating on the Garter Ceremony.*

*The Garter Ceremony, Windsor Castle.*

The commentary position itself is historic. It is a window in the Chantry Chapel, from which Catherine of Aragon is said to have watched the Installation of Knights of the Garter, and from which Queen Victoria certainly did watch the marriage of her son, later Edward VII, to Princess Alexandra. Still in mourning for Prince Albert, she was dressed from head to foot in black. The date was 10th March 1863.

Now, 105 years later, little yellow lamps glowed on the choirstalls below me and the Banners of the twenty-six Knights of the Garter, red, blue and gold, hung unfurled above them. It would be hard to imagine a more graceful or historic scene with, above it, the beautiful carved roof, originally made by John Hylmer and William Vertue between 1506 and 1509. On either side of the altar lie Edward IV and Henry VI.

The Order of the Garter pre-dates the Chapel by some 130 years. It was founded in 1348 by King Edward III and is the oldest Order of Chivalry in Europe. At present, it consists of the Queen, the Prince of Wales, Queen Elizabeth the Queen Mother and twenty-three Knight Companions, each of whom is invested with his regalia by the Queen, who personally buckles on the Garter. Its derivation is said to come from a great Ball held after the capture of Calais, when King Edward picked up a garter, dropped by the Countess of Salisbury, and put it on his own leg. "*Honi soit qui mal y pense*," said the King. "Shame on him who thinks evil of it": the motto of the Order ever since.

On 28th May 1972, the Duke of Windsor died in Paris: the uncrowned King, who had reigned for less than a year in 1936. His body was flown to RAF Benson, and then lay in state in St George's Chapel until the funeral on 5th June. Fifty-eight thousand people filed past it.

It had been established, some months earlier, that BBC Radio would be allowed to broadcast the funeral service, but that television would not. It was, after all, a semi-private royal occasion with many cross-currents of personal emotion involved. I was a little surprised that permission for radio was given.

In view of the delicacy of the occasion I decided, as Head of Outside Broadcasts, to give the commentary myself. My reasoning was that I would get the blame anyway if anything went wrong, whoever the commentator might be. In fact, I was exceptionally busy at the time with other matters, including the organisation of the Olympic Games coverage, and was glad to receive a letter from Buckingham Palace afterwards, thanking me for the BBC's "sensitive handling" of the broadcast.

Due to a misunderstanding of timings, I found myself short of two minutes in which to set the scene before the service began. The coffin was to be carried from the Albert Memorial Chapel by a Bearer Party of Welsh Guards at 11.10 am. I prevailed upon the officer-in-charge to do this one minute late and then to gain a few more seconds, if he could, as the coffin was carried in procession down the North Aisle and up the Nave to the Choir. No slow march was ever slower. I gained the time needed and nobody was any the wiser for this little subterfuge.

The story of the Duke of Windsor ended where it began. It was here in St George's Chapel that, half a century before, as Prince of Wales, he himself had been installed as a Knight of the Garter. At Windsor Castle, on that December evening in 1936, he told the world that he had chosen to give up the throne for the woman he loved. Now his stall was empty, his banner removed, and a new young Prince of Wales was walking with Prince Philip and other male members of the Royal Family, behind his coffin.

It was carried past the little chapel where his reluctant successor, King George VI, lay buried, and then on to the Choir.

Here, the Queen, Queen Elizabeth the Queen Mother and the other royal ladies had taken their places. With them, in the front row of the Choir, was the Duchess of Windsor, the former American divorcee Mrs Simpson. It appeared to me that the Duchess was in a daze. She gazed vacantly around her, hardly seeming to realise where she was, or what was happening. She was comforted by those around her.

The coffin of the ex-King, wrapped in his personal standard, was laid on the catafalque, the red tunics of the Guardsmen making a vivid splash of colour against the dark oak of the choirstalls. It was an unforgettable scene.

At the end of the service, after the hymn *Lead us, heavenly Father, lead us*, Garter King of Arms proclaimed the styles and titles, including the words, "and, at some time, the most high most mighty and most excellent Monarch, Edward the Eighth". The Archbishop of Canterbury gave the Blessing and State Trumpeters sounded *Last Post* and *Reveillé*. Four Military Knights of Windsor then came forward to guard the coffin until it could be lowered into the vaults and taken later for burial at Frogmore.

I ended the broadcast with the words of the Queen: "The British people will remember him with gratitude and affection," and those of the Duke of Windsor himself: "Your country and mine – I wish it well".

Four years later, on 1st April 1976, I was outside St George's Chapel, in the Horseshoe Cloister, with its semicircle of timbered houses, as the coffin of Field Marshal Montgomery of Alamein was drawn through the gateway of the castle.

The long and impressive military procession had moved slowly through the streets of Windsor and now the gun carriage, pulled by six horses of the King's Troop, Royal Horse Artillery, had come to a halt at the bottom of the steps. A Guard of Honour of the Coldstream Guards, on the green lawn opposite, presented arms.

The coffin was draped in a Union Jack. On it lay the Field Marshal's baton, along with his famous black beret and his sword. This Knight of the Garter, who held "the hinge of fate" in his hands at El Alamein, had made his last journey.

*Field Marshal Montgomery*

Thirteen years before, I had sat with 'Monty' in the Chapel of St John's School, Leatherhead. It was during an interval between the rehearsal and the live television transmission of *Songs of Praise*. The Field Marshal was Chairman of the School Governors.

He and I were by way of being the stars of the show. Monty was to read the Lesson and I was to present the programme. We had both prepared for our respective roles. For my part, I had pasted my carefully-arranged notes inside a hymn book, which it would seem natural to be holding in my hand. Monty had arrived with two versions of the Lesson, both meticulously timed. The producer opted for the longer version. "Very good decision," said Monty.

During the rehearsal, I referred to my own school days. "What school were you at?" asked Monty when the boys had dispersed for their tea and we were sitting alone in a pew. I told him I was at Shrewsbury. "A splendid school," said Monty, "produced a number of good Generals". For the life of me, I could not think of one. Then, in a flash of inspiration, I remembered General Sir Bernard Paget who had been C-in-C Home Forces. "Ah, yes ... but Dempsey." General Sir Miles Dempsey had been G.O.C. Second Army in the invasion of Normandy. I waited expectantly for some revealing statement. "Very good cricketer," said Monty.

When I got home, I looked up the records and found that M.C. Dempsey had not only been Captain of Cricket at Shrewsbury, but had also played for Sussex. Monty seemed to know more about my old school than I did.

Here was a man of total lucidity and clarity of thought, quick at getting to the root of a problem or summing up a man with those piercing blue eyes. But also someone who cared desperately for his men and who wanted to get them home safely and quickly, with the war won.

He was a supreme professional in the art of war who, by his very presence, must have been worth a couple of Divisions. He enjoyed his fame but, unlike many others, he fully deserved it.

I will never forget those fifteen minutes I spent with Monty. I liked him very much in that brief acquaintance and even chided him gently for summoning the splendid General Sir Brian Horrocks, at that time commanding the 9th Armoured Division, in which I was serving, to be a Corps Commander in the Western Desert. He laughed. "We had to have the best, you know." And he got them.

Monty's wife had died in 1937 and he was a widower for nearly forty years. I felt that, despite his fame, he was a lonely man. Little did I know, as we sat talking, that I would describe his funeral procession thirteen years later. There was also something he did not know about me and which I think would have amused him.

My grandfather, on my mother's side, was a naturalised Englishman, who had come over to England from Germany, at the turn of the century, to seek his fortune in the wool trade.

His name was Rommel.

Wreaths of carnations, roses and daffodils, some shaped in the emblems of the Eighth Army or the 21st Army Group, lay on the grass on either side of the twenty-one steps leading up to the West Door of St George's Chapel. Monty's coffin was carried by young guardsmen of the Coldstream Guards. At its sides walked five Field Marshals, an Admiral of the Fleet, a Marshal of the Royal Air Force and Major-General Sir Francis de Guingand, Chief of Staff of the Eighth Army. At the top of the steps the Dean and the Military Knights of Windsor waited to receive it. Inside, the commentary was continued by Godfrey Talbot, the BBC War Correspondent at the Battle of El Alamein.

My part of the broadcast was over. From outside I listened to the service and to the final hymn:

> The strife is o'er, the battle done
> Now is the Victor's triumph won.

Field Marshal Montgomery was often accused of being conceited, bumptious, and sometimes rude. These things may well have been true at times. But he had, above all, one quality which those serving under him most desired and which makes comparisons with Nelson and Wellington valid: he was a winner.

Of course, there were many happy occasions, too, at St George's Chapel. My last broadcast there was of the moving service marking the sixtieth birthday of Her Majesty the Queen in 1986, held in the presence of twenty-three other members of the Royal Family.

I was inside and Brian Johnston was outside among the crowds lining the route from the Castle.

A rousing fanfare *Royale* was sounded at the West Door as the Queen entered. Then, as the procession made its way through the Nave, flooded by light from the Great West Window and led by the fine choir of St George's, the congregation of some nine hundred sang *Praise, my soul, the King of Heaven*, a favourite hymn on Royal Occasions.

That afternoon, children with daffodils sang a delightful song for the Queen in the forecourt of Buckingham Palace. In contrast, Queen Victoria, on her sixtieth birthday in 1879, was at Balmoral. A conjuror, we are told, came to the castle to do some card tricks for her.

I have a feeling that Queen Elizabeth II had the happier day.

# CHAPTER 19
# Our Speaker Today

The Chairman is on her feet and banging a gavel on the table.

"As you know," she shouts above the hubbub of gossip, "we always have the speaker before tea, so we can enjoy ourselves afterwards". Not perhaps the best introduction, but a choir and a sing-song follow the sandwiches and cakes so carefully prepared in the adjoining kitchen, so it may well be true.

It is a Group Meeting of Women's Institutes. For the uninitiated, this means that 176 women (I have spent my time on the platform counting them) from the eight Institutes in the Group have come together, in one of the larger village halls, for their biennial meeting.

The eight Presidents and myself occupy the stage. *Jerusalem* has been sung, raffle tickets sold and two ladies by the door are counting and re-counting the money. Each W.I. has made a report on its activities over the past six months. The Secretary, sitting next to me, reads the Minutes of the previous meeting; "Mr Hudson's fee was rather high, but it was decided to have him anyway; oops, I shouldn't have read that". Laughter all round. I try to look value for money.

I have already judged the competition. It consists of eight Royal Tableaux created with imagination and care. I commend the losers as well as the winner. It falls to me, too, to draw the raffle, the prizes for which repose on a table in front of the stage, and to present various other awards. Surprisingly, the winner of the 'Scrabble Prize' gets a silver cup. Oh, and there are still five seats left on the bus to the pantomime.

But now, my time has come. The long rectangular hall stretches into the distance. There is no microphone, so I will have to throw my voice for an hour to the furthest row. It is very hot. I have driven fifty miles to get here and the fifty miles back through the rain and darkness will seem much longer. Meanwhile, 176 women expect to be interested and amused. I place my watch on the table and rise to my feet.

The 'Gab Racket', as it is inelegantly called in America, took me by surprise.

It is much more widespread and professional than I had imagined. There is an insistent demand for good speakers. This new profession, to me anyway, beckoned on my retirement from the BBC staff in 1975, although I continued for many years after that as a freelance broadcaster.

My new-found freedom gave me time to help my wife with her growing activities in the world of antiques, in which she specialised in Porcelain. Sixteen years later, I found I had given eight hundred talks, in every county in England and many in Wales and Scotland. Long odds might have been laid against that.

The growth of Ladies' Luncheon Clubs has been a post-war phenomenon. Once a month, except in high summer, their members gather in one of the better hotels of their local town, arriving early to make sure of a seat with friends, a place in the car park and a sherry at the bar before it gets too crowded. Lunch is usually at 12.30 so as to leave time for the meal, coffee and at least three-quarters of an hour for the speaker who has meanwhile set an alarm clock to catch an early train to the North, where many such clubs thrive. Rising rail fares cause difficulties. "We need to have some local speakers to save money," says the Treasurer apologetically, but everyone is 'local' somewhere. Travelling a long distance does not make you better – just more expensive.

Our speaker will be armed with throat pastilles, a railway timetable, a warm cardigan and lecture notes carefully prepared for the task ahead. If he or she is wise, the size and average age of the audience will have been ascertained in advance. If slides are to be shown, they must fit the projector provided.

A committee member will be waiting at the railway station, unmistakably anxious eyes scanning the outpouring throng; relief in her face as you walk straight up to her. Outside in the car park, a well-washed car will speed you to the tryst. "Do you mind a woman driver?" No, certainly not; invariably excellent and safe.

Well-known TV 'personalities' will not bother with preparation. How lucky you all are that he has come – and what large amounts you will pay for a doubtful privilege. Shorn of script and autocue, he or she will often have little to say. "Just wanted to catch the train back – and first-class, too"; this is the Chairman speaking over the prawn cocktail. "Shan't have him again, I can tell you – and would you mind passing the bread?"

No broadcaster will find public speaking easy. His audience, hitherto unseen, now becomes alarmingly visible. He is aware of every member of it and of the different expression on each face. Some smile encouragingly, some nod in agreement, others remain stony-faced and uncomprehending. Some radiate animation and interest, others look so bland that you doubt your own sanity. Also, some faces are more attractive than others, so beware of dwelling on the better samples.

"When they close their eyes," says the Chairman over the roast lamb, "they are not really asleep, just resting," and "if anyone goes out, they will be collecting their children from school." How kind she is, wanting me to feel at ease and be a success.

So the chairs are turned round and the Chairman, having banged, tapped, and blown into the microphone several times, introduces me in the way I have suggested to her over the peach melba. "I will be very brief," she says; but a good introduction is important. I am to talk about 'The BBC and Great National Events' and the audience should be told my qualifications for doing this. Others hold forth, apparently, on travel, music, antiques, fashion, needlework, flower arranging and many other subjects – but we speakers very rarely hear each other, so criticism is perforce second-hand. "It must be awful talking to a lot of women" – this over the coffee. Not a bit of it. Women make an understanding, interested and sympathetic audience. Marginally better, perhaps, is the mixed and middle-aged occasion, when I can go well back in time, trigger old memories and include more about sport for the men: always popular.

Worst of all, as far as I am concerned, is the all male, professional or Company Dinner, organised by Joe Bloggs at the behest of the Chairman. I recall, with particular horror, a gathering of some four hundred salesmen, mostly under forty years of age, on a night out without their wives and replete with food and drink. My turn to speak came at 11.25 pm after six previous speeches of exquisite boredom, mixed with risqué stories – of which I know none and wouldn't tell them if I did. I was in the wrong place at the wrong time. Never again.

Best of all, in my view, are the Lecture Societies who meet solely to hear a good speaker on a subject which interests them. Usually there is an interval for coffee. Often I have been asked to speak for forty-five minutes on either side of it. The audience is mixed, intelligent and experienced. This suits me well. No heavy meal is involved and the bar, if there is one, is sparingly patronised. All the work involved in preparation and travel is worthwhile because the audience is so clearly interested.

Let us consider how such a happy outcome can be achieved.

As in broadcasting, capture the audience in the first minute, preferably by laughter. They are terrified of boredom and, by all accounts, have had some unnerving experiences of it. Then, hold them firmly with a mixture of interest and humour – one or the other and all the time. No flagging, no let up, or you will lose them.

My notes are my stepping stones to salvation. Six postcards tucked into an inside jacket pocket, each one with a few headings to lead me in the right direction. They will suffice for an hour. Each subject is underlined in blue, each anecdote ringed in red; that way I can see a joke coming and slip it in, poker-faced, when they least expect it.

Avoid artificial signalling of the "that reminds me..." variety; stories must emerge naturally from the context of the talk. An expectation of amusement is created, but when and where is uncertain; so they keep quiet and listen intently. Now use your more serious, but always interesting, material. Speak, as far as possible, from your own experience – don't repeat what is public knowledge.

At first, I was nonplussed by silence, relieved when it exploded into laughter; later I came to recognise it as a compliment and devoutly to be wished: "Never heard them so quiet, usually they fidget and whisper," said one Chairman. "They were afraid of missing something," said another. So silence and laughter are your twin goals. But, primarily, your job is to entertain in the widest sense; light relief should always be just round the corner. A speaker without a sense of humour is doomed from the start. Use laughter to take a sip of water and glance at your watch and your notes. People love to laugh.

I like to speak for at least forty-five to fifty minutes, more if possible, but most Chairmen play for safety. "About thirty-five to forty minutes and then some questions," they will say. Questions are usually a waste of time; better to stay behind for a while and listen to individual hobby-horses: "How do you measure the size of the audience?" is a favourite one and "do you have to prepare for a broadcast?" is another. Yes, two solid weeks for Trooping the Colour. Votes of thanks are almost invariable, but superfluous. The speaker will know if he has been a success. If he hasn't, a vote of thanks is a contradiction in terms.

Halls, theatres and hotel dining rooms come in all shapes and sizes. Without a microphone, you may need to swivel your head to each corner in turn and even project your voice into the alcoves, but with a microphone, life becomes much easier, providing it works and you know how to use it. Most people speak too close to it, causing distortion. As a general rule, speak about four or five inches away and don't move your head while you are speaking; use a normal level of voice and let the instrument take the strain – that's what it's there for and given the chance it will save you from laryngitis.

On several occasions I have given two talks on one day at opposite ends of the country; once ending up in Hull, as a last-minute substitute, to address the Literary and Philosophical Society on the wrong subject, half an hour late and in a lounge suit instead of evening dress. I had been redirected from a lunchtime date at Kingston-on-Thames, by the indefatigable Kay Whalley of Foyles Lecture Agency, to whom I am much indebted. To be a substitute is not altogether a disadvantage as the audience is so pleased to see somebody, even if it is not the advertised speaker. They are on your side from the start.

Travel by train whenever you can. Nobody will pay you for wearing yourself, and your car, out. The trouble is that many places nowadays have no railway station. If you have to go by car, ask for a sketch map of the town or village, showing the exact position of the hall; verbal instructions are invariably hopeless. Enquire, too, if there is a car park, and ask for soap and towel to be available. At a W.I. meeting, the Gents' Cloakroom is, for obvious reasons, empty, but also often lacking in home comforts, badly needed after a long journey.

I am a firm supporter of British Rail's Inter-City service and even of their food, which has vastly improved but is expensive. The station buffets at Preston and Doncaster are my homes from home. Other regular interchanges take place at Peterborough and Newark to the East and of course at Crewe on the Western route. Many a cup of tea has been drunk at Grantham and Rugby. Living in St Albans, my starting points are Stevenage and Watford for the North, and Luton for the Midlands; but the most attractive line is down to the South-West, especially between Exeter and Newton Abbot, when the train runs parallel to the water.

British Rail, good as it is, can play tricks on you. February weather is to be avoided. Snow on the line caused me to arrive with the coffee at Preston, where I plunged into the Masonic Hall, wild-eyed, covered in snow, and wearing gumboots. At Bournemouth, after an engine failure outside Southampton, with no buffet on the train, and too late for lunch, I was given a very large whisky on an empty stomach. My talk seemed to get better and better.

An overnight stay means either a hotel or 'hospitality'; best of all is the hotel in which you have given, or will be giving, your after-dinner speech or lunchtime talk. More often than not, though, the cost of this luxury is too high and one finds oneself learning the geography of a hospitable, but strange, house. The danger here is that, if friends are invited in for drinks, one can end up giving the talk twice.

Some things are beyond your control. I could not be blamed for the lady who fell off her seat in a dead faint and lay prone in the gangway; nor for the teamakers, in the adjoining kitchen, who dropped a trayful of cups and saucers with a terrifying crash, in the middle of my description of a State Funeral. Nor can I help that elderly lady, so obviously sitting in a draught, or another one groping for her handkerchief, which has fallen on the floor.

To be a good speaker you must have something to say and be able to say it well. Some have one attribute but not the other.

The perfect speaker has yet to be invented.

He or she would arrive on time, neatly dressed and with impeccable manners. Such a person would make witty conversation before and during the meal – a duty I skilfully avoid, even if I could do it, by asking questions instead of answering them. This preserves the voice, without which nothing will happen. Finally, the talk would be a balanced blend of interest and humour, delivered to exactly the right length and for a most modest fee.

It was Max Robertson who introduced me to the strange world of the 'Lecture Circuit'. I am indebted to Margaret and Eric Nicholson of the Speaker Finders' Agency for arranging my first booking: a 'tea club' in Carlisle. Afterwards I was given a huge bouquet of flowers, a thing that has never happened since. My wife had visions of starting a florist's.

Speaking is comparatively well paid, especially if compared with BBC freelance radio fees. On successive days, I broadcast the Cenotaph Service 'live' from Whitehall to an audience of about two million at home and many more overseas, then spoke at a Ladies' Luncheon Club in the Midlands, where the audience was one hundred and five. The fee for the latter was higher.

Since my wife died of cancer, I have directed many of my fees to the Cancer Relief Macmillan Nurses Fund, to which royalties from the sale of this book will also go. So it has all become very worthwhile.

Do I enjoy speaking? Yes – provided the audience enjoys listening, and I have certainly been lucky in that respect. It is difficult work. You must be fit, on top of the job and tailor your material to the occasion. It has some of the fascination both of live broadcasting and acting. You speak largely off the cuff, as in a commentary, but your audience is visible, as on the stage. Not being tied to a script, you match material to mood, adding here, subtracting there, as time and your judgement dictate.

Your skill alone will hold their attention for an hour or so and make or mar their day.

Easier than broadcasting? No, in some ways more difficult. Adrenalin does not course through the veins in quite the same way as in a live broadcast, but a visible audience presents special problems which broadcasting does not.

It does not surprise me in the least that there are so few top-class speakers about. Some have an interesting tale to tell, but can't tell it; others have 'the gift of the gab', but nothing of interest to say. It is only when you get the two combined: a good story, well told, that you are on to a winner.

# CHAPTER 20

# Outlook Unsettled

It is symptomatic of the television age that, each year, about seven thousand viewers end up in hospital.

A woman fell head first through the set in her haste to switch on her favourite programme; one young man leapt so high in the air, when England scored a try at Twickenham, that he cut his head open on a chandelier; another punched his set with such vigour during a boxing match that he ended up in the casualty department of his local hospital. Unluckiest of all, perhaps, was the man so overwrought by a harrowing drama that he was attacked by his own Rottweiler.

We seem to spend our lives watching screens. All those sharp young men with braces in stockbrokers' offices, doing unimaginable deals by telephone; the girl at the check-out, each item displayed and the addition done for her; anxious passengers on a cold railway station, gazing hopefully at a screen hanging from the roof of the platform. And of course the author (but not this one) tapping away at his word processor.

As I write, in 1992, the shape of Broadcasting in Britain is changing. The money men are moving in, avid for huge profits. The sports authorities are relishing their new-found ability to play one TV organisation off against another in multi-million pound deals.

Unless we are careful, we shall go the way of the United States. Everything, good or bad, crosses the Atlantic. If so, this will mean a multi-channel diet of quiz games with one impoverished Public Service Network, inadequately financed by subscription. My American friends in California pay the equivalent of twice the BBC licence fee just to keep their sanity.

So the outlook is grim, unless we realise the danger. Broadcasting, both radio and television, may be driven relentlessly down-market by the need to deliver large audiences to advertisers. In all this the BBC stands like a beacon of hope, but also a beleaguered fortress.

It is over seventy years since the BBC took to the air in 1922. The licence fee then was ten shillings (fifty pence). As I write it is eighty pounds. That sounds a lot and, if paid in one sum, it is. In fact, it is twenty-two pence per day. A first class stamp costs more. In 1992 no national newspaper costs less than twenty-five pence. The *Daily Mail* is thirty pence and the *Daily Telegraph* half as much again.

During question time, after one of my talks, I suggested to the audience of about four hundred that the licence fee was the biggest bargain in Britain and invited anyone who disagreed to put their hand up. Nobody did. Admittedly they were middle-aged and roughly in the middle of our new 'classless' society, but it was a revealing moment.

Much of the potential income never reaches the BBC. About one person in fifteen flouts the law; a luxury hotel with perhaps three hundred bedrooms, each with colour television and radio, needs only one licence.

When the BBC Charter comes up for renewal in 1996, a Conservative Government will have been in office for seventeen years. It is the Government of the day which sets the level of the licence fee and gets very annoyed when the BBC bites the hand which feeds it. It is the job of the BBC and all broadcasters to question the actions of any Government. In my time, the loudest blasts of irritation came when Labour was in power!

In 1947 I was, for a short time, the only Conservative Councillor in North Battersea. In general, I have supported Conservative policies. However, it seems to me that privatisation has become a ludicrous mania. Some activities are no doubt better privatised. Others have their value, to the community as a whole, squeezed out of them by the profit motive.

Over the years, the BBC has been investigated many times, in a vain attempt to prove it inefficient, and thus unworthy of the licence fee, which the Government regards as a tax. We seemed to be permanently infested by members of this or that Commission. To their surprise, they found very little to complain about.

The BBC is held in world-wide respect by other broadcasting organisations. It began the first public television service in 1936. One thousand pounds was available for the first week's programmes. By today's prices that would pay for about nine seconds of a modern television drama.

The organisation of the BBC is widely copied; countless broadcasters from the Commonwealth have attended its training courses. Expatriates plan their lives round the World Service. Visiting BBC broadcasters are snapped up by local programmes overseas.

At home, the BBC is regarded sometimes with annoyance, but predominantly with indulgent affection. Ask the housewife permanently tuned to Radio 4, or the music lover to Radio 3 – even if it is occasionally interrupted by *Test Match Special!* The golfer sees the Open Championships from his armchair. Rugby Internationals come into your home for a tiny fraction of the cost of a ticket – even if you could get one. Add the Promenade Concerts, Opera from Covent Garden, *Yes Minister, Songs of Praise* and *The Forsyte Saga*, and the variety of the riches at your disposal over the years becomes apparent. Most telling of all perhaps, is the fact that the nation habitually turns to the BBC on National occasions, in a ratio of at least two to one.

Perhaps the BBC does too much. Was it right to go into Local Radio? Are five radio networks too many?

It is a 'Catch 22' situation. If the BBC ignores these responsibilities, its role as Britain's leading broadcaster and its share of the audience will be at risk. Attempts will be made to deprive it of the licence fee.

If the BBC's share of the audience falls below about 40%, which it almost certainly will, in the face of increased commercial competition, pressure will mount again for some networks to be financed by advertising. This would destroy the ethos of the BBC and the Corporation has rightly set its face against it. The only viable possibility, in my view, is that advertising might be taken on Radio One, which, in a sense, is a law unto itself with a very large and youthful audience. Sponsorship of certain programmes is another alternative.

Fault can always be found with any large organisation and the BBC is no exception. The size of its staff is often used as a stick with which to beat it but, in relation to its widespread commitments round the clock, this is not excessive. Criticism usually arises when large numbers of BBC staff turn up at political Conferences. This is due to overlapping of departments, which has certainly been a weakness in the past. The fusion of News and Current Affairs will have helped this.

The BBC must now 'contract out' twenty-five per cent of programmes to independent companies. Why this should be cheaper, or better, is not clear.

Many of these independent organisations are run by ex-BBC staff anyway. They certainly won't be doing it for less than their BBC salaries; more importantly, the standard of excellence, endemic to programme-making within the BBC, will be missing. A right-wing Conservative deplored to me the 'guaranteed income' available to the BBC through the licence fee. But only with such a guarantee can long-term programme plans be made. For example, the great drama productions, of which the BBC has been justly proud in the past, take time to script, cast, rehearse and produce. They are extremely expensive but bring a matchless quality to the screen – and to radio as well.

Most criticism of the BBC comes from people with no experience of it. To work in it as Producer, Administrator, Commentator and Head of an Output Department, as I have, gives quite a different perspective. We took a pride in public service broadcasting and in the programmes we produced. In administrative matters too we were remarkably efficient. The BBC's Staff Administration was a model of rectitude and fair dealing. On the financial front, I was personally proud of the fact that the Outside Broadcasts Department, whose budget could be knocked for six by an unexpected Royal Wedding or a run of England successes in the World Cup, almost always met its target.

Sports contracts will, I believe, play a big part in the future of broadcasting. The BBC and BSkyB are in an unholy terrestrial/satellite football alliance. When everyone has bought their 'dishes', they may have the additional pleasure of paying for sporting events by means of 'Pay-TV'. Unless the BBC can maintain its income, and so the power to bid successfully, the days of 'free' sport may be numbered. Without the sporting contracts, the BBC audience share will decrease and their right to the licence fee supposedly diminish.

Just as in 1936 the televising of King Edward VIII's abdication broadcast would have given the fledgling medium a shot in the arm, so, today, BSkyB must be desperate for further big sporting contracts. Events like Wimbledon would sell no end of 'dishes'. Let us hope the Lawn Tennis authorities stay true to the BBC, who first broadcast the Championships, on the radio, in 1927.

Paradoxically, BBC Radio may have a better sporting future than television. It is well liked and less expensive. The sports authorities tried, from time to time, to impose restrictions on us: for example by not allowing a broadcast of the first half of Football League matches. The truth is that very few potential spectators are kept away from a match by a radio commentary, however good it may be. BBC Radio, with the attendant billing in *Radio Times*, is marvellous publicity for any sport. Most realise that only too well.

With luck then, BBC Radio will be able to maintain exclusive sports contracts, even when commercial radio is nationwide, as it soon will be. BBC Enterprises, the commercial arm of the Corporation, is raising revenue through sales of programmes overseas, books, videos and tapes. Now it is set to sell time on the air between 2.00 am and 6.00 am for subscription and non-subscription programmes, made by independent contractors. All this will help.

My first contact with the BBC was in 1946. My wife-to-be had joined on her eighteenth birthday, during the War, in 1942. We met in the Outside Broadcasts Department in Manchester so, naturally, I am prejudiced! Joining the BBC in those days was rather like being accepted by a Guards Regiment or a London Club; OBs were the Household Cavalry. Nowadays, the BBC is but one of a proliferation of broadcasters bombarding us by satellite and cable; using the military analogy, some of its senior officers are now being posted to it from dubious second-line regiments. The BBC ethos will crumble and die if its senior management has not come from within. So far, despite its financial constraints and in relation to its vast commitments, standards are being reasonably maintained.

Pronunciation and clarity of speech have deteriorated however. The regular trained announcers, many of them women, are excellent, but there are so many voices on the air that they inevitably reflect a general sloppiness of language. Nowadimean?

News reporters, in far-flung and dangerous places and armed with modern technology, perform prodigies of accuracy and valour. At the commentator's art, journalists fare less well. More recognition should be given to those behind the scenes: for example, the producers of great drama series, and the editors, not the readers, of the News. Script writers of top quality, particularly of comedy, still seem in short supply. Just a few are outstanding. An actor is nothing without a script.

The money men, and their attendant newspapers, will no doubt rub their hands in glee if the BBC is allowed to waste away, but 'market forces' alone do

*John Reith*

not produce the richness and diversity which makes life worth living. On the other hand, in a competitive market, a so-called 'personality', of limited talent and mystifying public appeal, can rocket to stardom and riches. In that deliciously apt phrase, such people seem 'to rise without trace'.

The BBC has contrived to be the widest and most trusted disseminator of News, the leading Patron of the Arts, the greatest Stage for Drama, the classic source of Comedy, a leader in Religious Thought, the National Sports Arena, and the Focus of Unity on Public Occasions.

The piercing eyes of John Reith, the tall taciturn Scot whose blueprint for Public Service Broadcasting, in 1922, led to these remarkable achievements, must be looking down with alarm on the current broadcasting scene.

If 'Auntie BBC' is your favourite Aunt, be vigilant. She is under threat.

# Bibliography

Briggs, A. *The BBC. The First Fifty Years*. Oxford University Press, 1985.

Day, R. *Grand Inquisitor*. Weidenfeld and Nicholson, 1989.

de Manio, J. *To Auntie with Love*. Hutchinson, 1967.

Wood, R. *A World in your Ear*. Macmillan, 1979.

# Acknowledgements

Photographs were supplied by the following:

Roger George Clark

The Hulton-Deutsch Collection, The Hulton Picture Company

Camera Press Limited.

BBC Photograph Library

S & G Press Agency

The cartoons were drawn by Peter Coombs

# INDEX